SWIMMING TEACHING AND COACHING

LEVEL II

EDITED BY RICK CROSS
and CHARLIE WILSON

Published by ASA Swimming Enterprises Ltd
1993

The Amateur Swimming Association
Harold Fern House
Derby Square
Loughborough
Leicestershire LE11 0AL
Telephone: (0509) 230431 Fax: (0509) 610720

First published 1993
Copyright © ASA, 1993
ISBN 09000 52 260

Series Editor: Rick Cross
Technical Editor: Charlie Wilson
Illustration: Peter Cullen
Cover design: David Allton
Designed by: Rick Cross
Printed by: Echo Press Ltd, Loughborough

Wherever the pronoun "he" has been used it should be interpreted as applying equally to men and women as appropriate.

Contents

3

PART VI – Competitive techniques

PART VII – Additional information

Preface

The publication of *Swimming Teaching and Coaching – Level 1* in this series, raised the profile of the unified and graduated approach to the notion of a teacher/coach "profession". Clearly, in view of the thousands of volunteers who work in sport, the definition of "professional" is more a matter of integrity and knowledge, rather than necessarily in terms of being paid. *Level 1* was an attempt to bridge the gap of "What is a teacher? What is a coach?" On the whole this concept has been largely welcome, certainly far more welcome than that usually afforded to changes in long established practices and traditions.

The overriding difference between the two aspects of the "profession" is more often noted in the quality of the individual teacher/coach, rather than the nature of the title. Good coaches are about improving quality and, therefore, provide appropriate feedback to their swimmers, including comment concerning technique, workrates and workloads, training regimes etc., in order to achieve their objectives. Bad coaches might well simply shout more loudly about the shortcomings of their swimmers, or just increase training schedules etc., with little or no accompanying feedback and, thereby, reinforce errors by constant repetition without the essential constructive comment. So, too, it is with teachers. The good ones will note that technique is sound over shorter distances, say, a width, and offer their swimmers a greater variety of demands and challenges with appropriate feedback. The weaker teachers simply either do not recognize the need for the variety of demand, or increase the demand with no comment. No matter what the title they work under, teacher or coach, the good ones are doing the same thing – not only setting out to improve the quality of their swimmers' performance, but actually achieving it, be they non-swimmers or potential Olympic Champions.

The above debate concerning a more structured approach to the question of the unified teaching/coaching "profession" has been sharpened considerably by the current debate on proposals for restructuring the whole of the ASA Teacher/Coach education and training process. In current, everyday life there is an increasing demand for quality and the monitoring and control that goes with it. The teaching/coaching "profession", again, not necessarily equating to payment, will not be immune to these demands for quality. We hope the two books in this series will assist the thousands of people involved in the improvement of those who either want to learn to swim or whose aspirations go far beyond that stage.

Rick Cross

*After qualifying at Loughborough, Rick Cross taught in a wide range of schools before becoming an LEA adviser and, later, head of teaching studies and in service education in a college of higher education. He is now a freelance lecture/consultant in education and recreation. Rick has served on a variety of ASA and ISTC committees, including being the Chairman of the ASA/ISTC Joint Working Party reviewing the whole of the ASA structure for teacher/coach education and training and its relationship with the introduction of National Vocational Qualifications. He is currently the Chairman of the Board of Directors of the Institute of Swimming Teachers and Coaches and is also an ASA Principal Tutor. He has edited two other books on swimming, including the **Level 1** book in this series, and is the author of **How to Coach Swimming**.*

Charlie Wilson

Charlie qualified at Loughborough and taught at Bedford Modern School until 1990. He is still Head Coach to, and founded, the very successful Modernian Swimming Club where many international swimmers have been produced. Charlie was also a founder member, and first president, of the British Swimming Coaches Association. Charlie is also a member of the FINA lecturing panel and travels the world both talking and learning about swimming. He is a former GB and Olympic Coach, an ASA Senior Coach (Swimming) and Tutor (Swimming) and has been tutor, assessor and director of ASA Teacher and Coach Certificate courses since the mid-sixties. Charlie is a member of the ASA Swimming Committee, Chairman of the Coach Certificate sub-committee, a member of the ASA/ISTC Joint Working Party reviewing ASA teaching and coaching qualifications, a member of the Board of Directors of the ISTC and its Technical Director.

PART I

HUMAN GROWTH
AND DEVELOPMENT

Introduction to Part I

Teachers/coaches constantly need to be conscious of the vulnerability of the young people with whom they work. Part I considers the areas of knowledge which teachers/coaches need to understand if they are to work safely with those in their charge, namely, the personal and physical development of the young. It contains a reminder of their expectations of the teacher/coach, and points to the importance of over exploiting young swimmers – simply because they are enthusiastic and willing. The trust they put into teachers/coaches should not be over-used or abused.

Chapter 1

Child Development

Dr Colin Lee

'Without a clear understanding of children, we become teachers of CONTENT rather than teachers of children'

Gallahue D.L., (1976)
Motor development and movement experiences for young children, Wiley

Introduction

This chapter explores some of the aspects of child development which influence the effectiveness of swimming teaching and coaching. To maximise this effectiveness, the teacher/coach must be aware of more than just what a child can do – there must also be knowledge and understanding of why a child is like s/he is.

The complexity of human development

As a child gradually progresses towards adulthood, there is an emergence and expansion of the abilities and capacities which enable him to meet life's demands. The child develops physically, intellectually, socially and emotionally, and, while it is possible to examine each of these aspects individually, it is important to recognise the extent to which they are interlinked. For example, a child may be an early maturer in the sense that s/he has greater strength, height and co-ordination than others of the same age. Whilst this can have advantages in terms of physical performance, it may possibly present disadvantages where social relationships are concerned.

When considering an individual child it is necessary to consider the child as a whole, not just one aspect of its development. This discussion will concentrate on the pattern of physical development and its interrelationships with a child's social and emotional development. Less attention will be paid, in this instance, to the specific development of intelligence and personality, but this does not imply a denial of their significance.

Physical development

This section will consider important aspects of physical growth and their relationship with motor development, i.e., the development of movement abilities and skills. While physical growth is a continuous and orderly process, individuals have their own rates of progress and the timing of key events, like learning to walk or the onset of puberty, varies from one individual to another. It is, therefore, necessary to understand the general principles of the growth process while always remaining aware of the variations which are present in any group who have the same chronological age.

General principles

As already stated, growth does not follow an even tempo. Rapid growth during the early foetal stage is followed by a slowing down around the time of birth. Growth then speeds up again in early infancy, only to slow down before accelerating yet again at the time of adolescence. The factors which can influence the quality and quantity of this growth include:

- maternal nutrition;
- possible smoking habits during pregnancy;
- nutrition;
- physical activity during childhood.

A prominent feature of the first two years of life is the striking progress made in developing motor control. Before a child reaches school age all the basic locomotor skills are normally established as well as a wide range of eye/limb co-ordinations. The major limitations on the capabilities of the average three year old are lack of experience (which either the environment or time itself have not yet provided), or the immaturity of a body structure, e.g., muscles incapable of the strength requirements of particular activities.

The newly-born infant has the body structures required for learning to walk but, until skeleton and muscles have matured sufficiently, walking cannot take place. However, these same body structures are mature enough for movement in water at an earlier stage. All the infant needs is opportunity, and this is dependent upon the environment actually providing this opportunity. Parental interest and the existence of parent and child swimming classes determine whether or not the infant has this opportunity for early swimming experiences – but the infant himself is physically ready.

It is known that physical activity is necessary for normal growth and physical development:

- the size and structure of bones can be positively affected by forces applied during carefully planned, safe exercise;
- the flexibility and strength of joints is maintained and can be extended;
- through exercise muscles are developed;
- there is increased strength and speed of action;
- the heart and lungs develop normal and desirable efficiency.

Swimming is a form of physical activity that promotes all these developmental features. Furthermore, there is evidence that swimming training during childhood can lead to increases in rate of growth. (Andrew G.M., Becklake M.R., Gularia M. and Bates J. (1972) *Heart and lung functions in swimmers and non-athletes during growth,* Journal of Applied Physiology Vol. 32, No. 2).

As far as children's motor development is concerned, the reasons for acquiring swimming skills at an early age are well-documented. The period from the age of eight years to adolescence is often referred to as the 'skill hungry age' – a wide range of specific physical skills can be acquired during this period when physical growth itself is progressing at a steady rate.

Adolescence itself is a period of rapid growth and it is also a time when regular, vigorous activity is especially important. Furthermore, it is a growth period which highlights once again the need for consideration of individual differences and needs. The timing of the onset of puberty is subject to wide variation. In girls it can be between 10 and 13 years of age, whilst for boys it is approximately two years later.

The first stage of adolescence is always the height spurt and differences between the sexes, which have been slight until this time, now become more apparent. During the years of primary schooling, teachers often comment on a slight superiority of boys in terms of overall skill development. The reasons for this are social rather than physical – skill acquisition, as such, has a high status in the male peer group. If there is a reverse situation in swimming, i.e., girls generally superior to boys, there are certain features of physical growth which may account for these performance levels. From birth, the skeletal development of girls is slightly more advanced than that of boys and this leads to potentially greater levels of biomechanical efficiency in water. There is the further phenomenon of females being prepared to work closer to maximum aerobic capacity than males. (Åstrand P-O. and Rodahl K., (1970), *Textbook of Work Physiology,* McGraw-Hill).

The physical differences between males and females are particularly influential during the female adolescent stage. The increased velocity in the growth of the skeleton and muscles (including the heart) means that there is greater potential for superior swimming performances by adolescent girls compared to that of boys who, although they may have the same chronological age, are still in the pre-adolescent period. The eventual differences in size between men and women are, to a large degree, due to differences in timing of the growth spurt during adolescence. The differences come partly because of the later occurrence of the male spurt, which allows for an extra period of pre-pubertal growth, and partly because of the greater intensity of the spurt itself. Upon completion of the adolescent growth spurt, males have a greater relative width of shoulder to hip than females, larger muscles, greater length of leg relative to trunk and a longer forearm relative to upper arm.

The differences in swimming performance between men and women are thus founded on the phenomenon of physical growth during adolescence. It is also true that such differences as exist between the sexes before adolescence are a combination of the factors already mentioned together with the socio/emotional consequences of the timing of adolescence in individuals, i.e., whether an individual is an early or late maturer. This has additional significance in terms of differences between individuals of the same sex and, before progressing to consider the relevant effects of social and emotional development, it serves as a further reminder of the need to consider each child as an individual, and of the interrelationship between different aspects of development.

Social and emotional development

Prior to adolescence it is very difficult to tell at a glance if a child is going to be an early or late maturer. For example, it is difficult to know whether a boy who is tall for his age means that he is a taller than average individual for genetic reasons or that he is maturing early. More indicators than height alone are needed to determine a child's stage of development.

Being an early or late maturer often has repercussions in behaviour. For young children physical size usually brings prestige. Boys advanced in development not only at puberty, but also before it, are likely to be leaders. Muscularly powerful boys, on average, mature earlier than others. Early maturers appear to be at an advantage emotionally; most studies of personality show that they are more stable, more sociable, less neurotic and more successful in society. However, they can also have their difficulties. There will be situations where the child's emotional development lags behind physical development. The physique may be of a young adult but the emotional ties are still with children. A girl of 10 or 11 years of age may, at the emotional level, wish to be with other children of the same chronological age, but if she has the physical development of some fourteen year olds this very fact may not only be a source of embarrassment but also of rejection by the less mature 10-11 year olds. In assessing a child's stage of development, therefore, observations of physical size must be combined with an awareness of constant features and sudden changes in an individual's behaviour.

Children's social development is significantly influenced by the stage of emotional development reached and the effect that has on social relationships. There are also many social influences upon children which often determine which types of skills have the highest status. Family, friendship groups and school are all potential influences on the skills which are acquired by an individual child. If the child perceives swimming to be a 'high status' activity, and if the child's environment provides opportunities to acquire the skills of swimming then, providing (and it is a big proviso) the learning process is successful, the child will become an enthusiastic swimmer.

A range of factors, therefore, determine the end-product and, if any one of these factors is negative, non-supportive or even 'anti-swimming', the child's attraction to the activity will inevitably be affected. As a child develops changes in the dominant social influences are often seen. Initially, the family's values and encouragements predominate. The young child's life is seemingly an unending series of new experiences. As each experience is repeated, the child learns a little more about how to react to that experience. Not everything is dealt with successfully, but where a situation is successfully mastered, the child delights in that mastery and self-confidence increases. This serves as a reminder of the importance of repetition of well-learned activities in a swimming lesson. Children need the reassurance that comes from the performance of things they are good at. Young children who know the 'ropes' about going swimming love the responsibility of showing newcomers how to deal with situations.

In the young child's world security is gained from the constants – the family, the routines, the same swimming teacher and so on, are all influences upon which the child is dependent. In the move towards independence it is often the case that, from around the age of nine or ten years onwards, the peer group becomes more influential. If a child's friends all go swimming, so will the child, but if the major interest among the friends is, for example, football, the child may be in a predicament. For most children, the ultimate determinant of their choice of activity is their level of success at the skills of that activity. If children are to continue to be regular swimmers it is obviously vital that their early learning experiences are successful. This, in turn, has implications in terms of the quality of instruction which they receive. Schools are probably more guilty than clubs to the extent to which the least skilled or experienced teachers are placed with children at the most difficult stage of learning, i.e., the non-swimmers and beginners, the very stage which requires the most skilled instruction. The long term implications of this policy may be considerable.

In addition to quality of instruction, the extent to which a child has successful learning experiences may be influenced by those physical factors already discussed. Furthermore, it is relevant to note that, when physical skills are categorized, it is usual for swimming skills to be classified along with gymnastics as skills of agility. This may provide useful insight into such sex differences as may exist between boys and girls in terms of sporting abilities and interests prior to adolescence.

Girls tend to significantly outnumber boys at primary school gymnastics clubs and, in the absence of hard evidence, it must be asked if this is due to peer group pressure or to a generally superior ability of girls to learn agility skills. If the latter is true, it would not be unreasonable to extend the theory to swimming. However, it is equally possible for a young boy to be a better gymnast than any girl of the same age, which not only casts doubt on such a general theory about learning but also acts as further reminder of the complexity of developmental factors!

During adolescence the body undergoes a range of physical changes which, while they are occurring, may influence rate of progress in skill performance to the extent that the rate slows down. The child who is expecting a constant rate of improvement needs to be made aware of such a plateau in performance so that its occurrence is not unexpected. In order to retain motivation during this period more variety in the learning situation can stimulate an interest level that might have waned if that situation had concentrated on a single area of expertise that had been emerging prior to adolescence. Once the adolescent strength spurt has started, the young swimmer's interest is re-stimulated by the accompanying improvements in performance.

In order to explain the differences between individuals it is necessary to consider the pattern of physical development, the influence on social and emotional development, the personality traits, intelligence levels and combined effects of all these factors upon the learning process. Such understanding arises from observations of the child both in and out of the learning situation. The teacher/coach must consider the child's physical attributes, social relationships, attitudes, aspirations and motivational state. Informal observations and conversations are often the only available 'modes of analysis', but they are nevertheless important sources of information which provide a clearer, more complete picture of the child. This, in turn, can increase the overall effectiveness of the teaching/coaching process.

Chapter 2

The Place of Competition in the Acquisition of Swimming Skills

Dr Colin Lee

Introduction

The general principles of the skill learning process are outlined in the *Level 1* publication in this series. However, the impact of the development of competitiveness, the place of competition in the learning process and the role of competition in the training programme, all need to be examined in more detail as aspects of the psychology of skill acquisition which can be greatly influenced by child development factors.

The one thing to avoid is a discussion of competition in an emotional context, and seeing it in terms of being a good or bad influence in the overall development of the individual. It would be naive not to agree with Rainer Martens (Martens R., (1978) *Social Psychology and Physical Activity,* Harper & Row) when he states: "Competition is a social process that is so pervasive in Western civilisation that none can escape it."

Educational debate during the 1980s gave prominence to the views of many educationists and politicians who argued that competitive physical activities provided through sport have no part in the educational process and should, therefore, be discouraged in schools. It is necessary to know that such a debate has occurred, but it should also be known that the National Curriculum in schools now clearly identifies a place for competition in school physical education programmes.

The swimming teacher/coach will be an influence on children's development – an influence which extends well beyond the physical exercise and training role. A growing body of literature is examining the role of the sports' teacher/coach working with children and concluding that children's social and moral development, as partial determinants of their personalities, will be influenced by the teacher/coach and the relationship between child and teacher/coach. Objective evaluation of both the development of competitiveness in individuals, and of the place of competition in skill learning and performance, is necessary if the effectiveness of instruction is to be maximised.

There is little research evidence with which to assess the theories of someone like Veroff (Veroff J., (1969) *Social Comparison and the Development of Achievement Motivation,* in Smith C.P., (Ed), *Achievement-related Motives in Children,* Russell Sage), who sees competitiveness emerging at approximately five years of age. Before it can begin children must have reached certain levels of cognitive maturity because the competition process requires an individual to have the capacity to direct behaviour towards an abstract standard or remote goal. Children must also be capable of self-assessment of performance – it is noticeable that a young child will seldom challenge another child to any form of competition unless the challenger knows that he can win! Thus, if competition is instinctive, the instinct is far stronger in some than others and will inevitably emerge at different times for different individuals.

The development of competitiveness is clearly related to the emergence of achievement motivation. It will be influenced by environmental factors related to:

- culture;
- family;
- peer group pressure;
- previous experiences.

High levels of achievement motivation may stem from anxiety, fear of failure, desire for mastery, desire for power over others or desire to exceed the performance of others. The skill learning environment will inevitably be a contributory factor in the development of these motives and traits and the swimming teacher/coach has to consider not only the extent to which the learner is apparently naturally competitive, but also the extent to which the actual selection of learning activities assumes, requires or contributes to the development of competitiveness.

In assessing the desirability and suitability of an element of competition in skill learning tasks, an awareness of the possible consequences of competition is vital. These consequences take three forms:

- effects within the learner;
- effects between learners;
- effects on performance.

The learner

What effect will success and failure experiences have on the learner, particularly when the learner is a young child? Experiential evidence suggests that it can produce both desirable and undesirable traits in the child's social and emotional development.

Success may lead to increases in self-esteem and self-confidence, while failure can have the opposite effect. 'Success' is meant as the achievement of the objectives intrinsic to the task. This, in turn, implies that the learner must, pre-performance, have a clear understanding of these objectives and then, post-performance, be clear about the extent to which these objectives were achieved. The role of the teacher/coach as a provider of feedback is obviously a crucial one.

Skilled and sensitive teaching/coaching is necessary if a child is to come to terms with experiences of failure. It can be argued that tolerance of failure is a necessary 'life-skill'. However, it is equally true that the ultimate objective of progressive learning in swimming is to build on success, and it is obviously necessary to evaluate children's failure and provide alternative experience in order to eliminate it. This does not mean that 'avoidance of failure at all costs' is the one and only objective. Where competition is an intrinsic factor in a physical activity, and often the source of its appeal, failure is an inevitable consequence for up to half the participants. The teaching/coaching task is to develop positive attitudes to failure by teaching the child how to learn from the experience.

One of the indicators of skilled teaching/coaching is the selection of tasks which match an individual's needs and abilities. The decision that the child will benefit from a competitive activity should be based on evaluation of the child's stages of learning and development. This leads to selection of the most appropriate form of competition for that child.

Between learners

Peer group influence on children from the age of nine years onwards has already noted that it can be especially strong in the area of physical skill development where skilled performance is a source of status recognition. It is the socialisation of the highly skilled which is most positively influenced by competition against others. Children with lower levels of skill will tend to avoid such competition if that is all that the learning situation has to offer them.

When competition is between children it is fundamentally important that competitors are as equally matched in ability as possible. This is both educationally and socially sound for it is evident that, after competition, competitors have a stronger attraction for opponents if they are of similar ability (Martens R., (1978) *Social Psychology and Physical Activity,* Harper & Row). This principle of 'equal competition' will be accommodated to a certain extent in swimming by the adoption of ability grouping. However, within the groups themselves there should be further matching of pairs or sub-groups of children so that, when competitive activities between children are included in the session, the maximum number of children actually benefit from the activity.

Competition's effect on performance

Numerous investigations supporting the contribution of competition to personal motivation and, subsequently, to performance (Singer R.N., (1980) *Motor Learning and Human Performance,* Collier Macmillan). Evidence suggests that competitive situations assist performance of well-learned and simple skills. However, it has also been shown that competition can impair performance on complex skills or skills not well-learned. It would appear that considerable practice of a skill is necessary before the learner's performance is actually improved by competition.

Such findings have important implications. The teacher/coach must consider the level of skill acquisition of the learner and the degree of task complexity or difficulty before deciding if beneficial learning will result from a competitive form of an activity. If it is assumed that a skill is 'well-learned' when the components of that skill are performed habitually, i.e., the movement patterns are well established, then competition provides a useful test of that skill. This can be a valuable diagnostic tool for the teacher/coach because any element of a skill which is not sufficiently established will almost inevitably deteriorate under the pressure of competition. In such circumstances it is obviously vital that the teacher/coach communicates to the swimmer precisely what has been learned from the performance, i.e., there are positive learning outcomes.

There may be evidence of such skill deterioration even in an advanced swimmer, e.g., in the latter stages of a distance race when the swimmer is combating fatigue as well as trying to respond to the competitive situation. In the training of this swimmer the emphasis is placed on the need to consciously attempt to maintain form. Conscious control of movement was something that was eliminated as the skill gradually became established so there is now a need to almost re-learn **thinking** about movement.

Competition is both a test of skill and a test of competitiveness. Its place in the learning/training programme of swimmers is governed by the teacher/coach's need to assess both the performance and the performer. It is essential that there is positive learning from the experience and much depends on the learner's understanding of the purpose of the competitive activity. It is, therefore, important that the teacher/coach communicates the value which s/he places on the activity, and this can arise from the form of competition being introduced. In the teaching/coaching of swimming there are five potentially useful forms of competition.

Performance against personal standards

The most significant form of motivation in all skill acquisition is self-improvement. At all stages of learning this should act as the major form of challenge. Personal standards may be measured in terms of distance, time or form but, whatever the criterion, if teachers/coaches place sufficient emphasis on the value of self-improvement, the learning progression will have an invaluable foundation.

In the early stages of learning swimmers are usually aware of their own progress. In the intermediate stages, when swimmers are usually acquiring and refining the skills of specific strokes, the need for confirmatory feedback is vital – all too often swimmers themselves are unable to tell, from just the feel of movement, if they are making progress and the teacher/coach's observations are vital. Swimmers gradually accumulate a series of 'Personal Bests' (PB), e.g., the teacher/coach's 'marks out of five' for a mushroom float or a timed one mile of Butterfly. The knowledge that a 'PB' has been exceeded can act as a powerful motivator in circumstances which otherwise could have been de-motivating. Self-competition is the first form of competition that the swimmer should experience and it should have a prominence throughout all learning and training. It ensures that swimmers have the possibility of 'winning' whenever their swimming skills are tested.

Performance against established norms

The feedback of information about performance is an important influence on skill acquisition. This feedback can be internal or external. The former involves both the actual 'feel' of movement and the extent to which an intrinsic goal within the task is achieved. Young swimmers have rarely developed the ability to set goals for themselves and skilful teachers/coaches should adjust challenges to meet the needs of each individual.

External feedback can take a variety of forms, e.g., performance-analysis by the teacher/coach, or the tangible reward of a badge or certificate. The look of joy on the face of a swimmer receiving his first certificate is sufficient justification for award schemes, but such schemes are most wisely used as a resource to be integrated into the total programme of swimming skill learning, rather than as the sole determinants of content. Challenges must be geared to the stage of learning and distance is the predominant measure of progress in the minds of most beginners. As skill develops so, too, does the attraction of the challenge of speed but, throughout the early and intermediate stages of skill development, some deterioration of skill is to be expected. This deterioration can result from fatigue, or as a simple consequence of trying too hard. How the swimmer responds to these challenges can be an indicator of the individual's level of competitiveness. A carefully graded series of performance norms is provided for swimmers by the Rainbow Awards and, at a later stage, the Speed Swimming Awards. The teacher/coach should assess each individual's readiness to achieve standards prior to testing so that there is a very strong likelihood of success, an essential experience in the first stages of skill development.

Competition against other swimmers

The remaining forms of competition involve swimmers in competition against each other, i.e.,

- performance against another person;
- performance within a group but against other members of the group;
- performance within a group against another group.

It is important to reiterate the need expressed earlier for such situations to be based on a principle of equal competition within the learning/training environment. Nothing is gained from the race between unequally matched swimmers.

Competition between swimmers can be a fun element in sessions but, for children, and for most adults, it is only fun if there is a reasonable chance of winning. To the teacher/coach falls the responsibility of assessing the swimmer's readiness for competition and then deciding upon the most suitable form of competition for that swimmer. Self-competition is most appropriate in the early stages of learning, while the other forms can be introduced gradually when they will have a usefulness for the swimmer and/or the teacher/coach. The essential principle is that of 'readiness', and teachers/coaches must recognise the folly of placing the swimmer in a form of competition which is inappropriate to his skill level.

The learner is most likely to come back for more if he leaves a session with an overall feeling of having been successful, and there are a variety of ways of achieving success.

PART II

PHYSIOLOGICAL ASPECTS
OF PERFORMANCE

Introduction to Part II

The impact of exercise on the human being needs careful thought, particularly if the humans concerned are young. However, no matter what the age, it is essential that the teacher/coach background in these matters is such that it enables them to take sound decisions which reflect an understanding of the outcomes of those decisions. Gradually, across all sports, the great advance in teaching/coaching has been the movement away from, "How can I make my swimmers work harder?" to "How hard should the swimmers in my care be working?" The "Make it hurt, make 'em sweat!" era is over. More consideration is given both to the needs of the individual's lessons, programmes and schedules as well as the stage of development of that individual. Part II raises some of the points which will increase the teacher/coach understanding of these issues.

Chapter 3

Physiology of Performance

Michael Peyrebrune

Introduction

All swimming movements require energy provided by a complex breakdown of foodstuffs within the body. There are a number of related processes which take place before this movement takes place and they can be explained at a microscopic and sub-cellular level. These processes make up the metabolism (chemical changes) within the human body. The processes which initiate movement and allow the continuation of movement can be broken down into four discrete areas:

- neuromuscular control of movement;
- muscular contraction;
- re-synthesis of energy through the three energy systems;
- activity of the cardio-respiratory system (heart lungs and circulation) during exercise as a support for the energy production process.

Neuromuscular control of movement

The human body is able to move by a complex system of muscles and levers. The levers are the bones of the skeleton and form a rigid frame with which to make definite movements. The muscles are the tissues which can change their length, thereby creating a force to move the levers and allow movement to take place. Despite this ability, the muscles themselves need signals to determine:

- when to contract (usually shorten);
- when to relax, (usually lengthen);
- which muscles should contract (depending on the nature and direction of movement required);
- the force of contraction.

This control of skeletal muscles from the central nervous system (CNS, consisting of the brain and spinal column), is described as "voluntary", i.e., the human body is consciously aware of the movements being made. Once the brain has decided and initiated the movement, nerve impulses travel through the spinal cord to stimulate the motor neurons (nerve fibres) and thus deliver the information for contraction to the specific muscles. A motor unit contains the motor neuron and the muscle fibres it stimulates; it may control several muscle fibres or several hundred, depending on the size of the muscle group and its necessity for sensitivity. When the stimulus from the neuron is transmitted **all** the muscle fibres associated in that motor unit will contract. This is known as the 'all-or-none principle'.

Nerve Fibres

Nerve tissues are described as 'excitable' as they react to changes in their electrical potential. Throughout the length of the nerve the membrane surrounding it acts as a control point to ensure changes in electrical potential can be made by altering the content of sodium and potassium ions. When the nerve is stimulated the action potential is created with a 'knock-on' effect, transmitting the information down the nerve fibre to the connected muscle fibres. Within a muscle the force of contraction is regulated by the number of motor units recruited and the rate at which they are stimulated. The combination of these two factors allows the body to increase the intensity of effort during swimming movements from light to maximal. The selection of the correct motor units in the correct muscle groups, as well as their stimulation rate, is part of the complexity of the CNS which results in establishing movement patterns within the system. If repeated sufficiently, exact movements can be replicated time and again under all manner of stresses through an ingraining process in the CNS. This is one of the important reasons for repetitive training with good technique on specific strokes.

Motor Units

The ability of a motor unit to be recruited depends on its characteristic of contraction speed. The motor unit acquires its characteristics from the type of muscle fibres the motor neuron serves. These fibre types and characteristics are represented at Fig. 3.1.

Figure 3.1 Classification and characteristics of Motor Units in human skeletal muscle

Type of motor unit	Metabolic characteristics	Rate of contraction	Force created	Fatigue rate
Type I	Oxidative	Slow twitch	Small	Low
Type IIa	Oxidative/Glycolytic	Fast twitch	Medium	Low
Type IIb	Glycolytic	Fast twitch	Large	High

Key: Oxidative = Oxygen is used to metabolise foodstuffs for energy production
    Glycolitic = Glycogen is the sole fuel for metabolism, therefore anaerobic (without oxygen)

This information has an important relationship regarding swimming performance, namely, that sprinters should possess a greater proportion of Type IIb muscle fibres in order to facilitate work at high speeds in the shorter distances. Distance swimmers should possess a greater proportion of Type I fibres in order facilitate success in the longer distance events through better resistance of fatigue.

Fibre Recruitment

One of the most important factors regarding the recruitment of the three types of muscle fibres involves the intensity of the exercise. If the swimming intensity is light, and predominantly aerobic, Type I fibres will be recruited. As the intensity increases above the anaerobic threshold (transition from predominantly light to predominantly heavy exercise), Type IIa fibres are recruited. If the swimming speed increases further, and intensity approaches high sprinting levels, Type IIb fibres will be recruited. This additional recruitment will lead to the faster fatigue rate which is associated with the contraction of Type IIb fibres.

Muscular contraction

In each muscle of the body there are thousands of individual muscle fibres. The muscle, together with its fibres, is contained in a connective tissue (protective casing). Within each muscle fibre are many myofibrils. These contain the protein filaments (Actin and Myosin) which are responsible for the shortening of the muscle and, therefore, the resultant movement. When a motor unit has been recruited the excitation caused by the neuron is transferred deep within the muscle fibres and, in the presence of energy, causes cross-bridges to develop between the protein filaments.

Although muscle fibres have been stimulated electrically, they need energy in order to create the movement of the protein filaments. This is provided in the human body by the breakdown of a high energy compound called adenosine tri-phosphate (ATP). It is the splitting of the phosphate bonds within this compound that provides the energy for muscular contraction.

Muscular contraction and training

Physiological changes within the muscle after training can be seen in both the tissue itself and the nervous control of the muscles. Training studies have discovered significant increases in protein within the myofibrils (particularly myosin), as well as overall increases in size and number of myofibrils within each muscle fibre. This muscle fibre hypertrophy (increase in size) is usually associated with strength training regimes. In order to accommodate this muscle hyperthropy (and, therefore, the potential contractile force) increases in the quantity and strength of the connective tissues have also been observed. Training adaptations in the neural system include more efficient muscle fibre recruitment, allowing more economical movement through better co-ordination, and also better contraction rates reducing any excess contractile force.

Correct swimming movements, therefore, should be repeated regularly, and some training should be done at the same speed of contraction as those experienced during competitive races. Land conditioning should also at times try to mimic the same movements and speeds as those experienced under competitive conditions in the water.

The three energy systems

Adenosine tri-phosphate (ATP) breakdown provides the human body with the energy required for muscular contraction. However, there is only enough of this compound stored in the body to allow exercise to last for only two or three seconds. The ATP which has been broken down to adenosine di-phosphate (ADP), or adenosine mono-phosphate under extreme exercise stress, needs to be replaced or built up to its original form before energy expenditure and, therefore, muscular contraction can continue. The body has three mechanisms for regenerating the ATP compound:

1. Creatine Phosphate (CP) which is stored in the muscular cells is broken down providing the 'missing' phosphate band to reconvert ADP to ATP;
2. Glycogen or glucose (simple carbohydrates) is broken down 'incompletely' without oxygen (anaerobically) through twelve enzyme linked reactions, with the subsequent formation of lactic acid;
3. Carbohydrates, fat or protein in the presence of oxygen (aerobically) are broken down 'completely' through a series of complex biochemical, enzyme-aided pathways to carbon dioxide and water.

The relationship between these energy systems and their associated terminology is illustrated in Fig. 3.2 on page 24.

Figure 3.2 The three energy systems (defined)

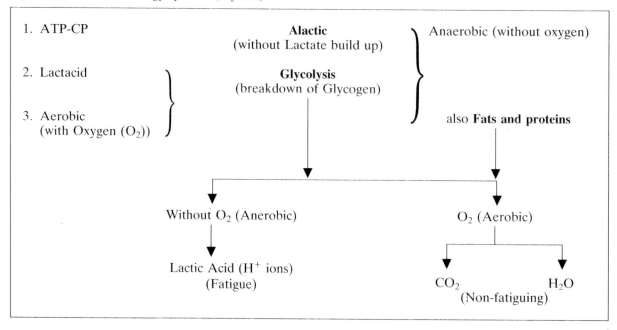

These energy replacements are important considerations in both training and competition. The swimming-time continuum and the intensity of the swimming effort will be affected by the speed of energy replacement required, the type of energy store available and the quantity of that store. Fig. 3.3 describes the characteristics of each store:

Figure 3.3 Characteristics of the three energy systems

System	Fuel used	Chemical & biological reactions required	Speed of replacement	Quantity of store
1. ATP-CP	CP	One simple reaction, within muscle cells	Very fast	Very small (<10 seconds)
2. Lactacid	Glycogen	Twelve enzyme aided reactions, within muscle cell	Fast	Medium (approx 1 hour)
3. Aerobic	Glycogen Fat/Protein	complex set of enzyme aided reactions. Transfer of oxygen from air-lungs-circulation-muscles	Slow Slowest	Medium (approx 2 hours) Large (weeks)

24

From the swimmer's point of view the intensity and duration of the effort are vital. If the energy is required immediately, and at a fast rate, as in a 50 metre sprint, the ATP-CP system will provide the majority of the energy requirement, backed up towards the end by the lactacid system (or anaerobic glycolysis). If the energy is required at a slower rate over a longer period of time, as in an endurance training set, the desired energy source would be through aerobic metabolism which is non-fatiguing (see Fig. 3.3). If a high percentage of fat was burned as a fuel a 'sparing' effect of glycogen could be achieved. In both circumstances the body would still be able to produce a sprint or series of sprints after the set by not having depleted its 'fast rate' (CP and glycogen) energy stores. Fig. 3.4 shows the approximate time courses for the respective energy systems.

Figure 3.4 The time course of the three energy replacement systems

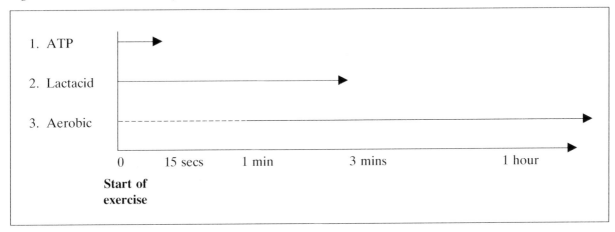

There are many examples of the relative break down of percentage energy contribution from each system during the competitive swimming races (see further reading). These vary somewhat between authors, and may account for individual differences such as:

- percentages of each muscle fibre type;
- the training background of the swimmer (long term);
- the current training status of the swimmer (short term);
- gender
- age/maturity differences.

At all times it is important to consider the duration and intensity of swimming, not the distance. An Olympic competitor may be able to complete a set distance in half the time of a young age group swimmer.

Improvements in the efficiency of each of these systems can be achieved through training, details of which are included elsewhere in this book. Fig. 3.5 on page 26 gives an approximate guide to the type of training which will improve the efficiency of each system.

Figure 3.5 Diagrammatical representation of guidelines for intensity duration and rest in interval sets for training the three energy systems

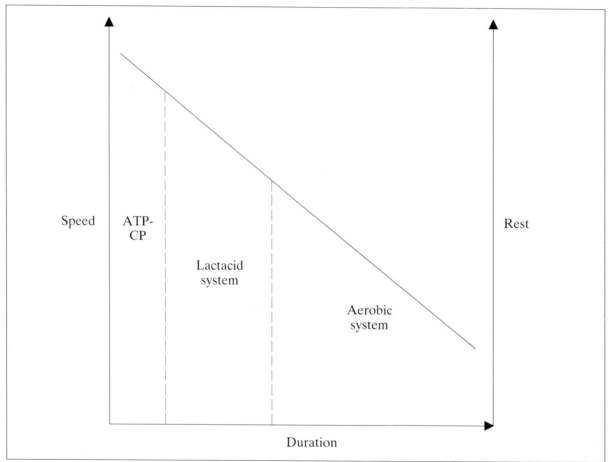

The cardio-respiratory system

The cardio(heart and vascular)-respiratory (gas exchange) system is the oxygen transfer mechanism which supports aerobic metabolism. The system transports oxygen-rich blood from the lungs for use by the working muscles and delivers carbon dioxide-rich blood from the working muscles for exhalation at the lungs. During exercise many metabolic changes take place within this system to satisfy the increase in energy demand. At the onset of exercise receptors in the muscles, joints, tendons, arteries, lungs and brain detect chemical, sensory, metabolic and mechanical changes within the body. As a result, ventilation rate and depth, as well as heart rate and heart beat contraction force, increase. Blood vessels to the working muscles and skin dilate to allow greater oxygen transport, and aid the thermo-regulation of the body respectively. The great extent to which changes in the system accommodate the increased demand for energy can be seen in Fig. 3.6.

Figure 3.6 Example values of selected cardio-respiratory functions at rest and during exercise

Cardio-respiratory function	At rest	During exercise
Heart rate (beats per minute)	50–70 beats	180–200 beats
Stroke volume (amount of blood pumped by the heart per beat)	60–80 millilitres	120–180 millilitres
Cardiac output (amount of blood pumped by the heart per minute)	4–5 litres	20–30 litres
Ventilation (amount of air breathed per minute)	8–12 litres	120–180 litres

The body makes these acute changes under exercise conditions, but it also makes longer term adaptations to these stresses and it is the latter adaptations that we hope to enhance through endurance training.

Cardio-respiratory changes induced by training

Cardiac output can be improved significantly through endurance training. This is a function of stroke volume and heart rate (see Fig. 3.6). Heart rate at maximum work rates will not change significantly, although it decreases at given submaximal intensities (a sign of improved cardio-respiratory efficiency). The increase in cardiac output after a training programme is due to the improvement in stroke volume. There are two reasons for this:

● the heart as a muscle, increases in size (hypertrophy) and develops a more powerful contraction enabling it to force out more blood per beat;
● the heart improves its ability to re-fill its chambers (pre-load) more fully after each contraction. If it can contract with a greater quality of blood to start with, the blood pumped out of the heart will also be greater. This situation relies on improved venous return (return of de-oxygenated blood from the working muscles). After training, the body is able to improve venous return as the working muscles which surround the blood vessels are stronger and better prepared to squeeze the blood vessels on contraction, thereby helping to pump (a 'second heart') the blood back to the heart.

Training over a period of time will also enhance respiratory functions. Ventilation per minute will be improved through an increase in lung volume (and, therefore, the amount of air inhaled in one breath) and also through an increase in breathing frequency. The diffusion capacity (the amount of oxygen that can be transferred from the surface of the lung to the red blood cells in the blood) will also be improved, as will the working muscles' ability to extract the oxygen from the blood vessels.

Measurement of the cardio-respiratory system

The adaptations previously discussed will all contribute to the body's improved ability to transfer oxygen from the air to the working muscles. This can be measured by calculating oxygen uptake through gas samples. It follows that the maximal amount of oxygen a swimmer can transfer to his working muscles per minute (VO_2 max) will be an accurate measure of his cardio-respiratory (and therefore endurance) ability. A strong linear relationship exists between oxygen uptake and heart rate and the measurement of pulse beats during training has proved a popular method for the assessment of intensity during endurance swimming sets.

Traditionally, maximal oxygen uptake has been used as the best measure for the assessment of aerobic capacity and the prediction of success in endurance races. Although it is still a valuable indicator, more recent studies have found stronger relationships between endurance ability and the ability to maintain swimming speeds at a high percentage of their maximum oxygen uptake. Gas analysis measurements are awkward and cumbersome and other methods for the assessment of this intensity have been sought. The relationship between various blood lactate indices and swimming speed is now one of the most commonly used in conjunction with appropriately designed field tests.

Chapter 4

Methods of Water Training

Charlie Wilson

Introduction

In this chapter both traditionally and currently accepted names for methods of training have been avoided. The aim has been to describe the methods with principles in mind. With a plan established, with a balance of training decided, with assessments made and with a purpose in mind the execution of the training plan is the next step.

Warm-up and preparatory exercises

No matter what the level of performance, learner to Olympian, some form of preparatory exercise is essential. In competition it is referred to as **warm-up,** at lower levels of activity it becomes **preparation** or even **introductory activities.** Whatever the name the objective is the same, i.e., **to prepare the individual physically and mentally for a task ahead** – immediately ahead if possible, though our systems of competition make this difficult to fulfil. Swimmers are often faced with hours of waiting between warm-up and competition. As time between warm-up and performance increases the benefits of preparation decrease. This does not mean that "long range" preparation has no value since such aspects as pool orientation are useful at any time. It is during a long waiting period that methods other than water warm-up come into their own. Much can and should be done on land and its value as a "re-warm" increases as the time gap grows.

Educating swimmers on the importance of warm-up is vital. It is not merely a matter of providing a set routine; swimmers must have a knowledge of principles so that they are more highly motivated to both warm up correctly and adapt to any conditions or unexpected situations.

Key points for all preparation

1. Before leaving for the pool check equipment.

2. Arrive for lessons, training or competition in good time to avoid the anxiety roused by haste and to allow time to become familiar with surroundings and routines.

3. A land stretching and mobilising routine suitable and/or adaptable for all situations is essential:
   - to warm the body so that it can then perform more efficiently;
   - to initiate the preparation of all physical systems;
   - to offer opportunity for mental rehearsal;
   - to reduce anxiety levels.

4. Water preparation follows, assuming that conditions are suitable. This has to be adaptable to allow for variations in time available as well as adverse and crowded conditions. There are three broad sections to the water warm-up:

- pool orientation and appraisal of pool conditions;
- various swims and/or water exercises to stimulate all systems and muscle groups to maximum efficiency for the task to follow;
- mental preparation to reinforce techniques and to focus on the task ahead.

5. The period following warm-up must also be planned to ensure warmth, comfort and reduced anxiety until the time for action arrives.

Warm-up exercises

1. Land exercises are covered fully in the chapter on land training.

2. Begin the water-work with a long, initial swim involving full strokes and drills for mobilising and for feeling that the strokes are at their best. Elements of turns should be included here.

3. Kicking exercise is vital. The kicking muscles are some of the biggest in the body and require specific attention. Kicking should begin easily and aim for full range of movement. This should be followed by short, fast bursts and finish with a return to easy kicking using a full range of movement again. The Breaststroke kick requires more care and should begin with an alternating action, followed by the full range of movement with force applied. Finally the full kick is applied as described above.

4. Race specific practices, including pacing swims, should follow to stimulate the areas of aerobic stress. Individual medley is an excellent way to produce the desired effect.

5. To complete the range of stimulation there must be bursts of maximum effort swims. A set of four sprints of 10 to 15 seconds, or their equivalent in distance or numbers of strokes, with rests of 30 to 50 seconds is minimal for this purpose. If more sprints are felt to be necessary the sets should be separated with relaxed swimming for about 5 minutes. This section should also include starts, turns and finishes. The **teacher/coach should observe and reinforce the various aspects with positive comment.**

6. The final phase should begin with recovery pace swimming and gradually reduce to calm, relaxed swimming during which the mental processes look back reassuringly through the warm-up and then forward into race imagery.

It is the duty of the teacher/coach to oversee, but not to dominate the warm-up. Swimmers who have been well coached to be self-sufficient do not need the constant ministering or interference of a teacher/coach. In the increasing tension and anxiety of the pre-race period the teacher/coach must show a calm confidence, and offer a reassuring presence, and not an over-zealous pressure. Sometimes it is apparent that the teacher/coach needs the swimmer more than the swimmer needs the teacher/coach. It is also the duty of the teacher/coach to instil correct behaviour during warm up. Fooling about in the lanes and standing about in the water at the end of the pool are not only poor procedures, they can also be a danger to others. Teachers/coaches who overlook this sort of behaviour, or fail to educate swimmers, also fail in their overall duty. Swimmers who cannot comply with the rules of acceptable behaviour should be reported to the warm-up marshal.

Purpose of training

All training must be purposeful and all concerned, particularly the swimmer, must know and understand at a level and in a manner appropriate to age, ability and aptitude, the purpose of the work. Lack of understanding and intellectual involvement are prime causes of demotivation and "drop out".

For ease of study it is convenient to separate the various areas. It must be remembered that the body as a whole is affected by any training, specific or general; total isolation is never possible.

Aspects of training
Technique training
Without sound techniques, training for performance becomes a pointless exercise. The performance development process is summed up in Fig. 4.1.

Figure 4.1 The performance development process

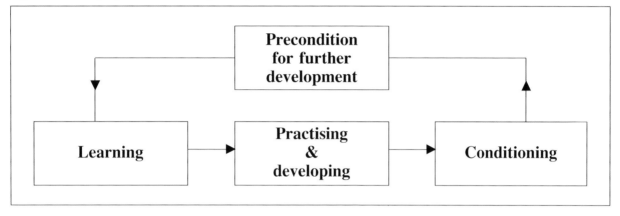

The first and last stages of the process, learning and conditioning, have been the subjects of an extensive range of literature. They are adequately covered, too, elsewhere both in this book and in *Level 1* of this series. It is those vital middle sections, practising and developing, which have become the poor relations. All too often swimmers, particularly young swimmers, are rushed from the learning phase into the conditioning phase with newly learned, but unskilled techniques. The three phases are compatible and blend easily, one with another. Many repeats of short distances (an aspect of interval training) leading to sub-maximal long distances (overdistance training) are the basis of technique development **and,** at the same time, aspects of conditioning. However, neither is an automatic outcome and there has to be conscious emphasis on one or the other for maximum response. In this section technique is the prime consideration; the various aspects of conditioning come later and are of secondary importance here. Only when techniques are fully grooved, and development is well advanced in the later years, will the roles be reversed. It bears repeating that **slogging up and down a pool against the clock is of little use if technique is poor.**

Drills
Drills are exercises and are often modified strokes. They are essentially a skill in their own right, but they are an excellent method of developing technique and are an important part of any training programme. Transfer of training is not automatic. Each drill has a specific purpose and this must be known and understood by the swimmer for any transfer to occur; without this understanding the drill remains a skill

on its own. Lists of drills have little value in themselves, though they are a source of stimulation and assistance to the teacher/coach. The process of using drills:

- assessment of need;
- communication of this to the swimmer;
- selection or invention of an appropriate exercise;
- communicate what the swimmer should aim to feel;
- ensure that the exercise is enjoyable and satisfying.

Example
1. Swimmer's timing in the Butterfly stroke is incorrect and he has insufficient arm endurance to practise over any distance.
2. Explanation of the timing.
3. Drill chosen is single arm Butterfly using fins.
4. Swimmer practises with no endurance worries and able to concentrate on the timing.

Stroke length and stroke rate

The most important aspect of stroke technique development is the manipulation of **stroke length** (SL) and **stroke rate** (SR). Stroke length is the distance the swimmer travels on each propulsive movement. Stroke rate is the number of strokes performed in a minute. In Front Crawl and Back Crawl a stroke is the complete movement of one arm; a stroke cycle is the complete movement of both arms. In Breaststroke and Butterfly stroke and cycle are the same. **All swimming training is directed through a combination of these two.**

The usual method of calcualting these factors is from a time and a number of strokes for a standard distance, e.g., 16 strokes for 25 metres is a stroke length of 25 divided by 16 or 1.5625 metres. However, if this is swum in 20 seconds the stroke rate is 60 divided by 20, multiplied by 16 which is 48 strokes per minute.

There are available stroke rate watches which calculate stroke rate from a count of three strokes. This type of watch is valuable because it allows a coach to monitor a number of swimmers within a relatively short distance. From an early age swimmers should be taught, then encouraged, to count strokes and take their own times. It is all part of independence and understanding.

SL × SR is an indication of the biomechanical efficiency of a stroke and, when combined with measurement of energy output, is an excellent guide to which type of stroke a swimmer should adopt in any particular situation. Efficient swimmers tend to fall between the extremes of two ways in which they swim strokes:

- high application of force, high degree of propulsion and high energy output per stroke, i.e., low SR high SL
- low application of force, low degree of propulsion and low energy output, i.e., high SR low SL.

The extreme towards which swimmers lean depends upon many factors concerned with physical and mental capacities, early teaching and technique quality. Human beings tend to practise activities they enjoy and find natural and comfortable. Swimmers do just this and train in a way most comfortable for them, sometimes to the exclusion of all else. Should they do this they will eventually meet a point of diminishing return because there are limits to the rapidity of arm or leg action, or to the amount of force which can be used economically or effectively. It is important that swimmers should practise all methods. This is not to change from the natural way of swimming, but gradually to introduce other elements in order to avoid reaching that sticking point of diminishing return. Modifications and practices should be introduced over a period of sufficient length to which will allow adaptation to take place without losing natural qualities.

Methods of developing SL × SR

- in the early learning stages stroke counting, self timing and experimenting with varying speeds of arm and leg action should be practised
- constant reference to the three above mentioned factors
- matching SL and SR to energy output
- stroke reducing exercises

Swimmers of high quality should be able to switch from one type of stroke to another in the course of a race, e.g., a high energy cost stroke rate may be inappropriate for the whole of a distance event, so choosing a low energy cost rate for most of the race and switching to a speedier high energy cost stroke for the latter part could be a good race strategy. This requires careful race practice and testing to decide when the "gear change" should occur. In age group swimming the consideration of stroke length and stroke rate is a most important part of training.

"Increasing the frequency (SR) only becomes worth pursuing when a swimmer's pull length (SL) is greater than twice the arm length. What is more, both the strength available and the swimming technique proficiency must enable this pull length to be maintained."

(Wilkie K., Madsen Ø., (1986), *Coaching the Young Swimmer,* Pelham Books)

Training the energy systems
Aerobic capacity (Basic swimming endurance)

This covers a very wide range of training, from swimming simply for mental and physical relaxation, and it includes maintenance of an efficient aerobic system for the purpose of recovery and enhancement of more stressful swimming. It also includes increasing the aerobic capacity:

- **"easy" relaxed swimming** has a place in training. It has value in neuro-muscular recovery after severe stress has been placed on the nervous system, in mental stress recovery and in providing time for mental preparation for effort. It is used as the final stage after recovery swimming and as a total recovery activity in sprint training (see below). The method of training really needs little emphasis physically and most swimmers, particularly more adult groups, need little encouragement to swim in this way. It is important to ensure that swimmers understand its value and that they have a catalogue of useful activities. Younger swimmers will require specific instructions on what to swim so that in later years they can readily understand the briefest instruction to swim easily or to relax;
- **recovery swimming** moves up the intensity scale. In terms of measurement, the lactate level for recovery swimming is 1.5 to 2.0 mml/l. Whilst this is comfortable swimming it is not easy, relaxed swimming. It is the level of intensity at which the aerobic system can most efficiently assist in the reduction of lactate levels after very intense activity. Energy system recovery is at least 50% more efficient when active recovery of correct intensity is used, rather than passive rest.

At least 5 minutes of swimming at this intensity should form part of every swim down or recovery but, if conditions do not permit this amount of time, even one minute is beneficial. It is best practised regularly, either as a swim down toward the end of training sessions or between repetitions and sets of high intensity. It is swum in sets and is followed by easy relaxed swimming. The type of swimming is described in the next section dealing with maintenance levels.

Teachers/coaches must be vigilant in ensuring that recovery pace is understood and used on every appropriate occasion.

- next on the intensity scale is **Aerobic maintenance.** The level of intensity is important for maintaining the efficiency of the aerobic system. The measurement of this is in the range from 2 mml/l lactic acid up to the so-called anaerobic threshold, or onset of blood lactate accumulation (OBLA). Methods of training for this system fall into two broad categories:
    - long continuous swims often referred to as over distance swims;
    - sets of shorter swims, or interval training, often referred to as extensive, or short rest, or even "slow" interval training.

Overdistance training

Overdistance is a relative term since the length of the swim depends upon the standard of swimming and/or the type of swimmer. Ten minutes could be an overdistance for a weaker swimmer or for a pure sprinter, with 20 minutes for the elite, middle distance or distance specialist:

- **Overdistance varied intensity** – this covers a range of swimming from so-called *Fartlek* through to controlled pace for race tactics. *Fartlek* is of Swedish origin and is lifted from the world of running. The spirit of *Fartlek* is important. Pace, swimming exercise (usually stroke), and even direction, where possible, are chosen as the individual feels. The only controls are time and/or distance. This type of swimming is for the older swimmer with a range of experience from which to draw. Younger swimmers require guidance and control, unless the swim is set with the specific aim of extending imagination and ingenuity. From pure *Fartlek* it becomes simply a matter of exerting more controls over distance, intensity and stroke according to the effect desired. Obviously age, training age, will power and experience play a large part in this type of swimming. To ensure that varied pace does not become constant pace change of stroke should accompany change of effort. Only highly motivated and experienced swimmers will be able to achieve more subtle pace change on one stroke.
- **Overdistance constant pace** – this includes a wide range of swimming from distances set for achievement (swimming awards) to "challenge" swims, through to carefully controlled pace swims for the experienced competitive athlete. Time, distance and stroke are the set controls, i.e., time for a set distance or distance for a set time, both with the stroke specified. When carefully controlled, this type of swimming is an excellent device for monitoring aerobic capacity.

Extensive interval training

This is a method of achieving the volume of exercise necessary for the maintenance of aerobic fitness and efficiency and, at the same time, offering maximum scope for following those two vital principles of **Adaptation** and **Variety** by juggling with the variables of **Distance, Repetition length, Time** and **Intensity.**

Features:

Length of set:	20 to 60 mins (2000m to 4000m) depending upon main event, training age and motivation
Intensity:	Up to anaerobic threshold (OBLA)
Rests:	Short, 10 to 30 secs (depending upon repetitions)
Repetitions:	50m to 800m

Extensive interval training is compatible with the learning situation, i.e., both consist of the repetition of patterns of movement at a sub-maximal, but controlled, intensity, with short rests and **with brief intermittent comment from the teacher/coach.** Controlling the intensity with some precision is an important element if it is to be sufficient to maintain aerobic efficiency. Because the volume of swimming necessary to train the aerobic systems is so high, variety is essential.

● **Aerobic capacity improvement** – this is the next important step up the intensity scale. The intensity for this type of swimming moves out of the comfort zone, at or just over the anaerobic threshold. In lactic acid terms this would be between 3 and 5 mml/l, with males being slightly higher than females. The object is to stimulate the aerobic capacity at its extreme range and just over for the necessary overload for adaptation to occur. It is much more a feature of the training of the older age group and adult swimmers.

Features:

Length of set:	30 mins (1500m-2000m)
Intensity:	On and slightly over anaerobic threshold
Rest:	30 to 60 secs
Repetitions:	100m to 400m

Work done by Robson M.W. and Howat R.C.L., *Developing Swimmers' Aerobic Capacities,* published in *Swimming Technique,* Vol. 28, No. 4, February-April, 1992, suggests that after 4 repetitions of 200m (4 × 200m) a recovery swim 1 × 200m is beneficial. Others have tried different ratios, but all agree that one or more recovery repetitions in a set is beneficial.

Intensive interval training

This is swimming well above the intensity of the anaerobic threshold and is often loosely described as **anaerobic training.** It is the method used to develop the anaerobic lactic acid system. Traditionally this has been known as "hard work" and teachers/coaches have devised various types of workout sets, each with its own special name and effect, real or imagined. All include certain essential features, only the balance of these changes.

Features:

Length of set:	30 mins (400m to 8000m)
Intensity:	Maximum effort for the repetition distance
Rest:	2-3 mins up to 10 mins depending upon the level of intensity achieved
	Rests are active at recovery pace, reducing to relaxed swimming prior to the next effort
Repetitions:	50m to 200m

In this type of training fatigue is high, both in energy system and in nervous system terms. Fatigue is also long term, with overtraining a danger. Recovery swims between repetitions and sets are essential, as are recovery days in the weekly cycle. Never more than three days of this type of training should be attempted in a week. The percentage of total training volume is low, say about 5 percent. Motivation to produce the necessary effort can be a problem. There are three basic sub-types of workout within this context:

● **Maximum anaerobic stimulation**

Repetition distances:	50m to 75m maximum effort
Rests:	2 mins to 4 mins active rest
Total set distance:	400m to 600m

An **essential is complete recovery after each repetition.**

Example

8 × 50m on 4 mins with 75m recovery pace and 75m relaxed swimming plus short passive rest for mental preparation.

- **Lactate tolerance**

  As the name implies, this is as much a mental exercise as a physical one.

  Repetition distances: 100m to 200m
  Rests: 3 mins to 5 mins active rests
  Total set distance: 400m to 800m

This is not a race pace exercise. Swims should not be paced, but should be afforded maximum effort from the start.

- **Speed endurance development**

  It could be said that this type of training belongs to the "Race Pace" section, but since all swims are so high in energy cost it is felt that they play a very important part in anaerobic development. However, the pace in Speed Endurance training is more controlled; it is a percentage of basic speed. The lap or repetition distance is specific to the individual rather than a group standard, and is determined by the Speed Endurance test. The measure of improvement is the increase in lap distance for the given speed, or an increase in speed for a predetermined distance. Rests between repetitions are shorter so that recovery is incomplete resulting in a steady stress increase as the set proceeds.

  Repetition distances: Determined from testing
  Rest: 1 min to 3 mins
  Total set distance: 200m to 800m depending upon individual ability to hold pace

Anaerobic alactic energy system development (sprint or basic speed training)

In energy system terms methods of training sprint or basic speed involve developing the anaerobic alactic system. Other factors concern the nervous system, reaction time and biomechanics with the efficient use of power. The anaerobic alactic system, often referred to as the ATP/CP system, delivers a large amount of energy per unit of time. The drawback is that the muscles' stores of creatine phosphate are used very rapidly, i.e., 4 to 7 seconds at maximum effort. The by-products, carbon dioxide and water, are readily dispersed and recovery and regeneration is near complete in about 45 seconds. There is considerable stress on the nervous system's motor units.

Features:

Length of set: Maximum 8 repetitions
Distance of repetition: Maximum 20 metres
Pace: Maximum
Rests: 30 to 50 seconds of **passive** rest or very gentle, relaxed swimming

The stress on the nervous system is considerable and can lead easily to overtraining. Between sets there should be at least five minutes of calm, easy swimming. Sprints can be straight or may involve starts, turns and finishes. Obviously the use of the pool width is valuable. The chapter on monitoring describes the measurement of basic speed, starts, turns and finishes. This is ideally suited to sprint training; the precise measuring, along with competition over widths, provides motivation to maximum effort.

Use of resistance and assistance

The same basic methods are employed in developing power by means of resistance or assistance. These methods are not suited to children.

Resistance methods
- using paddles or extra large paddles;
- using apparatus or clothing to increase drag;
- tethered swimming (a proven method involving swimming with a piece of shock cord or latex tubing with one end attached to the swimmer with a belt and the other attached to the end of the pool).

It must be emphasised that these methods are stressful, particularly to the shoulders, and long rests between sets are essential with much easy swimming. The training sessions immediately following must be of low intensity.

Assistance methods
- sprinting, being pulled through the water slightly faster than basic speed by some external force;
- sprinting, using self generated, but artificial force, e.g., fins.

Methods for reaction time development

These are principally for young age group swimmers below the age of twelve, the age most suitable for the development of the nervous system. It consists of very short, maximum effort, bursts involving a sharp reaction to signals. This form of training lends itself perfectly to game activities and competitions.

Race pace training

Methods of training for pacing involve not only hitting accurate times, but also precise control of stroke rate. Teacher/coach and swimmer must know the most appropriate stroke rate for any given race or part of race. This means careful monitoring during competition, assessment of technique and the energy costs of modifications. Timing the sections of a race, "splits", with the pacing relationships noted, is essential. These relationships are:

- even pacing – all laps same speed;
- "drop off" – the difference between sections when laps are progressively slower;
- negative split – second half faster than the first.

These are logged, along with changes in stroke rate, for possible adjustment/modification in subsequent training.

It is important to reduce drop off and to approach even pacing which is, for most swimmers, the most efficient and beneficial manner of racing. For this reason, practising negative split swimming is a valuable training device. It is possible, too, that some swimmers find negative split racing most suitable for their physiological make up, although the choice of appropriate pace and stroke rate is the vital and difficult decision.

There is a high degree of similarity between sets of repeats for pace training and for aspects of energy system training. If this occurs naturally then the situation should be exploited. Neither method should be compromised for the sake of the other. There are three main aspects of race pace training:

- race simulation – in which race situations are reproduced as closely as is possible in training;
- race conditioning – in which sections of a race are repeated at actual race pace or slightly faster to achieve overload;
- mental preparation – swimming in which confidence and understanding are built.

Race simulation

From the monitoring of races, and discussion with the swimmer, strengths and weaknesses are formulated. Plans can then be laid to build specific parts into the new goal. This is followed by practice. Over the years coaches have devised ways of following this method and have given names, such as **Broken Swims** or **Simulators.** It is essential that underlying principles are followed with an eye to individual needs, and not slavish adherence to fashionable methods.

As a race proceeds it becomes tougher both physically and mentally; holding pace means a concious increase in effort. A swimmer who merely holds initial effort feels comfortable, but the swim becomes slower. Race simulation, therefore, must reflect the increase in effort and must hold precise pace. This means that the increase in effort, making things tougher, must be made **not** by increasing speed, but by variations of rest between splits or by increasing the length of the split.

Example

Race goal is 4 mins 14 secs for 400m – this means swimming from a push off 100m in 1 min 04 secs. Initial simulation could be 8 × 50m with 20 secs rest at 32 secs. Subsequent simulation could move through 8 × 50m with 15 secs on to 8 × 50m with 10 secs then 6 × 50m with 10 secs, 1 × 100m on to 4 × 50m with 10 secs, 2 × 100m with 20 secs. The options are wide and will depend on the individual swimmer. If the race plan involves increasing pace in the later stages of a race then changes of stroke rate and stroke length can become part of the equation. Knowing how and when to change stroke rate and length requires very careful monitoring. Change in pace can be immediate, like a car gear change, or gradual over some distance or number of strokes; so much depends upon the individual physical and mental reaction to pace change.

Race conditioning

Race conditioning is closely allied to the types of training used for developing the energy systems. In this case, however, holding pace is the object, not holding set intensity levels. The two may be the same, but often they are not. Conditioning overload is achieved by swimming sets of repetitions in which each repetition is less than race distance and at a speed greater than race pace, the sum of repetitions in a set is greater than race distance.

Guidelines

	Lap length	Repetitions per set	Total repetitions	Rest
100m swimmers	25m	10	20–30	10–15
	50m	6–8	12–24	15–30
	75m	4	8–16	30–60
200m swimmers	50m	8–12	24–40	20–30
	75m	4–8	12–24	20–60
	100m	3–4	8–16	40–60
400m swimmers	50m	12–20	24–40	10–20
	100m	6–10	24–40	30–60

Rests between sets should be near complete to allow the building of maximum confidence.

Competition training

Competition training has two aspects beyond what has been said earlier;
- competition practice within a training session;
- the calculated use of organised competition as training.

Competition within a training session must follow race conditions as closely as possible. This can be anything from the full mirroring of a total competition with officials, and all the equipment, to isolated specific parts of competition, e.g., practising starts. No matter what is selected for practice the training must be exact. Mistakes allowed here will lead to mistakes in competition proper and so much disqualification, ill feeling and delay, particularly in starting races, could be avoided. The purposeful **exploitation of competition as training** for further competition, or as a test of some part of training, is not as widely used as it should be. This is not to encourage the deliberate losing of a race. The object of a race is always to win, and the only true way to try a new technique, or perhaps a facet of training, is to try to win with it in real competition. It is unfortunate that there are so many other pressures on swimmers which can distract from this important method of training. Swimmers and coaches have to be exceptionally single minded to follow new and unaccustomed race practices when instinct, and other pressures, tell them to win at all costs.

Sectional training

Strictly this type of training is in the drill classification, but it is so much a part of training that it needs specific attention. Sectional training is the isolation of the arm and leg actions for the purpose of specific development. It is usually referred to as **kicking** and **pulling.**

Kicking – It is unfortunate that all too often kicking has become synonymous with idleness and become used solely as a rest for the arms. Naturally, it is part of the cycle of work, rest and recovery and, in a cycle involving intense arm exercise, would follow that exercise, but this contrast with the arm exercise should be of incidental importance.

Efficient kicking is a vital part of all strokes and must be well developed. The leg muscles are some of the largest groups in the body and, therefore, take a considerable energy supply. In everyday life much of their function is weight bearing. In swimming the role is different, with mobility, pattern of movement and flexibility being the important aspects, not weight support. These contrasting, and in some respects unnatural, roles mean that they must play a considerable part in training. Volume of leg training must be high. They are trained using the methods described above, but one aspect which takes on great significance is the principle of **variety.** Ringing the changes in kick training is important, not only for developmental purposes and avoidance of boredom, but also for avoidance of overuse injury. Kicking must be made enjoyable to those who do not find it easy, but its use must always be purposeful.

Changing body position, or the judicious use of the arms, are excellent ways of reducing stress for those for whom kicking is difficult.

Fins provide first class assistance with kicking in the following ways:
- they provide enjoyment for weak kickers;
- they develop strength in kicking muscles;
- they help in increasing flexibility;
- they provide balance and support propulsion necessary for the development of some skills and drills;
- they assist in the development of basic speed and sprinting.

NB care must be taken as with the use of any equipment

Pulling – Most of the propulsion in swimming is from using the arms. It is advantageous, therefore, that they receive special training. Sets for arm training are the same as those described earlier, but with special care. Arms are under stress in all swimming, so it is essential in their specific training that cycles of intensity and rest are carefully planned.

- **Pulling using resistance**
  - paddles are useful in developing power in the pulling muscles; they also add considerable stress to an already heavily used joint complex. They should be brought into use gradually and never used when the shoulder joint is fatigued. There are three main types of paddle. The conventional paddle, just over hand size, the large power paddle and the arm paddle. All should be used in sets of short, fast repetitions. Claims are made for their use in stroke development, although this is doubtful. There is no use for hand paddles with young age-group swimmers except for fun, with fins as a balance.
  - various types of resistance mentioned earlier under **power development** can also be used to increase the overload on pulling. Again, **great care should be taken to avoid shoulder stress.**

Training formations

All too often training takes place only up and down the length of pool, in what is known as **chain swimming.** Teachers/coaches must consider the many alternatives.

Suggestions:

- chain swimming in lengths;
- use of widths;
- wave swimming (the formation used for competition!);
- circling the pool.

The very nature of swimming safely in large groups places constraints on the variations which may be used. It is essential, therefore, in the interests of variety and enjoyment, to make full use of the comparatively few which are available.

Chapter 5

Monitoring

Charlie Wilson

Introduction

Monitoring is about surveillance and discovering what is happening; this is a process which involves testing and assessing. Vague terms, such as "easy" or "hard" swimming, and the use of inaccurate and inappropriate methods of measuring are unacceptable. For successful teaching/coaching the accent must be on precise identification of training intensities, the ability to assess techniques objectively and the understanding of mental traits by the collection of data. Good teachers/coaches should be able to refer to their monitoring results and records to evaluate competition and previous training programmes so that further planning can take place with more certainty. Without monitoring teaching/coaching becomes guesswork.

This chapter is an introduction to monitoring and considers some of the more important issues:

- Individual profiles
- Technique
- Energy systems
- Speed and pacing

It could be said that the only valid test of performance is the result of the race or the water polo game or the synchro performance itself. A competitive performance, however, is a complex mixture of strengths and weaknesses as Fig. 5.1 suggests.

Figure 5.1 The complexity of attributes which combined to create performance

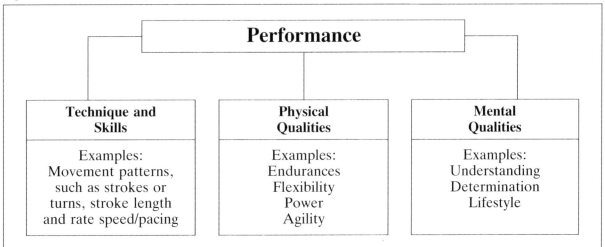

Improvement is best achieved if these parts can be identified, isolated, assessed and, if trainable, developed by training. Monitoring, that is evaluating and recording, is therefore a logical and essential part of teaching/coaching; it is part of the performance cycle. Knowing with certainty that methods of training are actually having the intended effect on the swimmer has always been one of the greatest problems teachers/coaches have faced. This raises questions which a teacher/coach must answer:

- What should be measured in order to evaluate and plan?
- What are the best methods of evaluation?
- Is it worth the time spent on it?
- How much information is communicated to the swimmer?

In former days coaching was even more a matter of "guessology" and "feel" than it is today. The more notable teachers/coaches tended to be simply good **observers** and good **communicators.** These two attributes, alone, are not enough, although they are paramount and must not be forgotten in the search for more accurate scientific methods. This "feel" method of monitoring is often founded on scant knowledge, long experience, the memory of trial and error and in teacher/coach personality. There is little that can be accurately measured or specifically identified, with the result that it is difficult to make comparisons; logical explanation is not easy and motivation, particularly with large groups, is a problem. All this, of course, adds to that air of mystery and secrecy which pervades some teaching/coaching.

Clearly, when accuracy is questionable, and fault identification a matter of guesswork, it follows that explanation of success or failure becomes difficult and relationships can easily break down. The combination of guesswork and the personality cult is not one to be followed. It bears repeating, however, that accurate observation and good communication are elements to be treasured.

Keeping Records

Keeping accurate records is part of the professionalism associated with monitoring. It is not only vital for "reference back", for the analysis and diagnosis of good or bad performance ready for future planning, but, also, it is the formal and accurate method of providing continuity of teaching/coaching from one group or teacher/coach to another. Monitoring records should be kept in the same way as school or medical records.

Teachers/coaches vary in their attitude to record keeping; it may reflect part of their personality and individuality and the way they feel about "paper pushing." The extremes are the problem areas. On the one hand the teacher/coach spends more time on meticulous, superfluous detail at the expense of personal contact and, on the other hand, the "back of an envelope" teacher/coach who, if s/he keeps records at all, keeps them on odd scraps of paper to be lost within minutes. In an ideal situation everything to do with performance should be recorded, but this is a vast undertaking and beyond the means of most teachers/coaches **if the teacher/coach tries to do it all personally.** Much can be done by club assistants on standard forms which can be brought to life by personal teacher/coach notes made through contact with the swimmers.

A comprehensive list of considerations for individual profiling is set out at Fig. 5.2.

Figure 5.2 Profiling considerations

Consideration	Notes
Personal details	Name, date of birth, address etc
Family background	Next of kin
Swimming Training details	Club, group, training age, times of training, strokes, standards, achievements, land training details

Aims and ambitions
   Personal Best Times
   Favourite strokes and types of training
	Strokes and distances

Medical background appropriate to swimming	Factors likely to affect both travel and performance. Hearing, sight, medication and allergies.
Education and/or work	School or work, demands on time, achievements and standards, aims and ambitions, likes and dislikes.
Any test results	Body measurements, including growth details. Earlier test results.

Notes
1. Teachers/coaches should be aware of the legal implications of keeping swimmer records.
2. Swimmers and parents of minors should be made aware that records are kept.
3. All records must be confidential.

Technique Monitoring

- **Pool side observation** – Stroke analysis with the teacher/coach on the poolside is the obvious form of monitoring. If stroke analysis sheets are standardised, and information is updated regularly, trends in stroke work can be monitored and developed more satisfactorily.
- **Video** – Monitoring by the use of video is even more useful, but it is essential that it is not indiscriminate.
- **Stroke Rate and Stroke Length** – The relationship between stroke rate and stroke length is one of the most important aspects of technique development. The use of this relationship has been examined in the chapter, "Methods of Training". However, the methods of monitoring need to be considered.

Swimmers, even at an early age, are able to undertake the necessary timing and counting and, with practice, they learn to do the necessary calculations. The process should begin as early as is possible in the teaching/ coaching stages before movements become too deeply grooved. It should be part of a swimmer's development to learn to count strokes and cycles, and master self-timing. It is, in fact, an early introduction to **understanding** – an essential part of the full development of a swimmer. Self help, when possible, is a vital part of monitoring. Apart from contributing to understanding and motivation, it is also useful for the hard pressed teacher/coach to be able to give swimmers responsibility for their own development. Teachers/ coaches are not secretaries, they should encourage their charges to perform some of these tasks, and so leave themselves free to analyse, interpret and advise. Perhaps youngsters will make mistakes, but that will contribute to the learning process. Furthermore, it is remarkable how accurate young swimmers can become when it is for their own good! By using simple materials, e.g., a soft lead pencil on a form of plastic sheet as a "slate", swimmers can record their own results after each attempt at a test. Results can be written on the plastic for the coach to collect and transpose later. "Writing it down" is an ideal way to focus the attention.

Stroke length is calculated by dividing a standard distance, usually a length of the pool (though purists would insist on eliminating the push off), by the number of strokes taken. **Stroke rate** is the number of strokes taken in a standard time, usually one minute. It is calculated either by using a special stroke/rate watch, or by counting the number of strokes for a short time, e.g., ten or twenty seconds, and converting into strokes per minute. Later, in a swimming career, these figures become very important in linking stroke technique with energy cost. In the early stages of development it is important to increase stroke length rather than stroke rate. Wilke and Madsen stated that, "Increasing the frequency (rate) only becomes worth pursuing when a swimmer's pull length is greater than twice his arm length" *(Coaching the Young Swimmer* (1986), Pelham Books). Stroke length, then, is the most important aspect to monitor in technique development in the early stages. The chapters on "Biomechanics" and "Methods of Training" will explain the "why" and "how" of development.

No matter what method is used to assess stroke technique teachers/coaches should aim to have as many constants as possible. Variations in speed and stroke rate will make comparisons unreliable. It is of little use trying to analyse a racing stroke in training unless it is swum at racing speed and at racing stroke rate. Two methods of achieving the constants necessary for comparisons are **Race Pace** and **Percentage Basic Speed.** The **Race Pace** method tends to be used more for older, experienced swimmers with a well grooved stroke pattern and a number of major races for a data base. The teacher/coach must have current lap splits and stroke rates of current races. It is then simply a matter of using these in stroke practice sessions swimming repetitions much shorter than race distance with rests sufficient to ensure that fatigue does not become a factor. If the effect of fatigue is part of the assessment then rests are shortened and the differences between rested and fatigued swims can be noted.

The **Percentage Basic Speed** method is one of particular value for the younger swimmer. In this basic speed is measured (described later) and stroke rate noted. A percentage, in fact 85%, of that speed is noted and the swimmer is asked to perform short repetitions at that speed for stroke technique purposes.

Example:
10m basic speed test is swum in 5.71 secs or 1.75 metres per second (m/s)
Assessment speed is 85% of 1.75 m/s, i.e., 1.487 m/s.
This will result in 25m in 16.8 secs.
The constant time for stroke technique laps of 25m becomes, therefore, 16 secs.

Monitoring effort or the Energy Systems

Since teaching/coaching for what has been known under many names, e.g., "fitness", "stamina" or "endurance", coaches have attempted to understand how to plan their training programmes accordingly, and to carry them out in the knowledge that they will be effective. The guesswork and mystery have been reduced by going from "How can I get my swimmers to train harder and longer than others?", i.e., the "no pain, no gain" brigade, to the latest and more relevant, "How hard and long should my swimmers be training for best effect?" To make this shift teachers/coaches **must** have a knowledge of human structure and development, anatomy, physiology and psychology. They must also **know** and **use** the basic training principles. Listening and copying so-called "top" coaches is of little value if basic principles are not constantly observed.

Monitoring can only really occur when the teacher/coach **understands what** is to be measured and **why**.

The energy system monitoring methods to be covered are, in order of increasing priority:

- Perceived Exertion;
- Pulse Rate;
- Standard Distance Swims;
- Standard Time Swims;
- Lactate Testing.

Perceived exertion monitoring

This consists of systematic observation of outward signs of physical and mental effort. Efforts have been made from time to time to rationalise and standardise methods by placing certain indications of fatigue levels in categories and forming a grading system. All this was to provide a system of comparisons. Outward and visible signs, however, are individual and their pattern, if there is one, is dependent upon too many factors to be reliable. So much depends, for example, upon a swimmer's relationships with a particular teacher/coach or other member of the group, e.g., observe a group reaction to a particularly tough swimming exercise when one swimmer, with particularly strong influence, decides to react badly; the rest are inclined to follow. Perceived exertion monitoring is in constant use in teaching/coaching, often without conscious thought. Teaching/coaching is a series of interactions between individuals and groups. The good teacher/coach registers the moods, the body language and all those small signs. If they can be noted and stored for future use that is even better. However, these observations are personal opinion, judgement and complex interactions. Teachers/coaches are human and can make errors of judgement based on their perceptions.

Pulse Rate

Heart rate has long been used as a method of monitoring effort. As effort or intensity of exercise increases so does pulse rate, and this obvious and well known relationship is easy to understand. Unfortunately, there is a great deal more to it than that. Its value has been grossly exaggerated and it can be an inefficient and ineffective method of monitoring, particularly at the higher intensity levels customary in swimming. The areas of concern are:

- At the higher levels, above 120 heart beats to the minute, counting manually by using the finger tips on a pressure point, is inaccurate;
- Changes in rate occur so rapidly after the cessation of exercise that it would be necessary to monitor during exercise – an expensive and time consuming affair;
- There are factors other than exercise which markedly affect the rate;
- Even if measured accurately on a one-coach-to-one-swimmer basis, interpretation is no simple matter if it is to be useful.

Areas where heart rate monitoring can be useful are:

- At very low intensities the lower heart rate counts are more reliable;
- At these lower rates of swimming a broader band of intensity is more acceptable. This is the type of exercise which is used in the development in the body's capacity to utilise lipid metabolism, i.e., the use of "fat" as a fuel;

- As an indication of general body state, as in overtraining or illness. In this situation the resting pulse rate can be abnormally high and/or is unusually slow to return to normal after exercise. Resting pulse rate is taken first thing in the morning before rising. Unusually high rates over two or more mornings can indicate that something may be wrong;
- In the general education of a young swimmer the knowledge of how the body responds to exercise is important. **Understanding** is a great motivator and heart rate monitoring, even if inaccurate for training purposes, is part of the early learning process.

Methods of measuring vary from the highly technical and accurate monitors attached to the swimmer during a swim which transmit to the teacher/coach, or to a recording unit; down through hand held battery powered monitors to manual finger tip monitoring. In the group situation the "finger tips" method is most widely used. The swimmer finds the pressure point and, using the pace clock, counts the number of beats in ten seconds. In swimming, pulse rate monitoring should be restricted to the areas specified earlier.

Standard Distance Swims

These are either **single distances** or **sets of repeats** which isolate, or are close to isolating, particular aspects of the energy delivery system. The total distance, the repeat length, the number of repeats, the resting interval and the intensity of the swim (the speed) are combined to place demands on one specific part of the energy system. The swims are often devised by teachers/coaches for particular conditions and particular swimmers and, if sound physiological principles are understood and followed, this type of testing is very effective. It is important, too, that they are carried out regularly following all the principles for testing described later. **Long distance swims,** beginning with 800 metres at an early training age, and moving up to 2000 metres, or even 3000 metres, at the elite late stage, are an excellent test of basic swimming endurance, i.e., the aerobic capacity. Tests must be swum at maximum effort and constant pace. This means that there must be a learning period, though experience shows that swimmers become adept at the test after two or three attempts.

Interval sets may also be used for the same purpose. As in the long distance test, the total set length will vary according to training age and ability. The aim is to improve the average time for the whole set.

Typical sets are:
20 to 60 × 50m with rests of 10 to 20 secs
20 to 40 × 100m with rests of 10 to 30 secs
10 to 20 × 200m with rests of 20 to 30 secs
 6 to 12 × 400m with rests of 20 to 40 secs

Improvements in time denote improvement in aerobic capacity. Aerobic tests should be undertaken regularly at intervals of three or four weeks and it should be remembered that **aerobic capacity** can change markedly over a relatively short period. A single distance test is used to measure speed endurance or **anaerobic capacity.** Interval sets are of little value in testing anaerobic values. This test is more complicated and need not be carried out as often as the aerobic assessments. In essence, the test consists of swimming as far as is possible at a very high speed, although, obviously, this is not precise enough to be valid. The speed needs to be constant, relative to current ability. A good speed to select is 90% of current basic speed (the basic speed test is described later). The pool is marked out at intervals of 5 or 10 metres. The swimmer, from a push off, swims at this basic speed with a timer checking the time at each interval marker. The distance achieved before the speed drops off is a measure of speed endurance in terms of distance.

Example:

Age of swimmer   18   Test distance   15 metres
Test time   7.7 secs
Test speed   1.95 m/s (rounded)
90% of test speed   1.75 m/s (rounded)

Target times for 10m distances in seconds

30m	40m	50m	60m	70m	80m	90m	100m	110m	120m	130m	140m	150m
17.14	22.85	28.57	34.28	40.00	45.71	51.42	57.14	62.85	68.57	74.28	80.00	85.71

The system becomes even more accurate if stroke rate is introduced into the calculations but, for most teachers/coaches in the club situation, this would be uneconomic in available time.

Standard Time Swims

The main influence in developing the energy systems is the time spent in swimming at the required intensity and the balance of the efforts over weeks, months and years. Measuring the intensity sustained over a period of time is an important and accurate measure of aerobic capacity. The so-called "T30" test, in which a swimmer swims for 30 minutes at maximum effort, constant pace and in normal training conditions, is one such measure of aerobic capacity. The time, of course, has to be adapted to "T20", "T15" or even "T10", according to the age, training age and ability of the swimmer. It follows the principle that if a swimmer, observing the conditions outlined above, swims for a time at the extreme range that his/her technique will allow, the swim, to use energy system terms, will correspond to that metabolic balance zone, the anaerobic threshold or onset of blood lactate (OBLA). The teacher/coach will have as a measure a speed which corresponds to the anaerobic threshold. With certain allowances for repetition distance and resting times the teacher/coach, utilising the speed calculated from the "T" test, can construct sets which are aerobic (slower), within the zone, or anaerobic (faster) than the anaerobic threshold speed. To calculate this speed divide the distance swum by the time in seconds and this will provide a speed in metres per second (m/s).

Example

Distance swum in 30 minutes is 2480m

2480 divided by 1800 (seconds in 30 mins) equals a speed of 1.378 m/s.

Times are calculated by dividing distance of training swim by the speed.

Using the above speed, a 400m time would be $\frac{400}{1.378}$ secs

or 4 mins 50 secs (rounded figure). This 400m time can be a useful reference point in constructing sets.

As mentioned above, allowances have to be made for repetition distance and rests when planning training sets. The table of percentages formulated by Dr. Ørjan Madsen *et al* (personal correspondence) has been found to be accurate for developing aerobic capacity. Sets of 400m with 30 secs rests use 99.3% of test speed, e.g.,

> Test speed = 1.4166 m/s
> 99.3% of test speed = 1.4067 m/s
> Target time is 400 divided by 1.4067, or 4 mins 44 secs

Sets of 200 with 30 secs rest use 102.2% of test speed

> 102.2% of 1.4166 m/s = 1.4477 m/s
> Target time is 200 divided by 1.4477, or 2 mins 18 secs

Sets of 100 with 30 secs rest use 107.8% of test speed.
Sets of 50 with 10 or 15 secs rest use 108.4% of test speed.

Overdistance swims should be swum at the test speed. This will be found to be tough at first, but it will improve aerobic capacity. Test conditions and administration should use the guidelines for testing at the end of the chapter.

Lactate Testing

This is a very accurate method of monitoring the energy systems in order to plan precise training intensities.

Lactate acid is always present in the blood. It is measured in thousandths of its molecular weight (90 grams) per litre of blood (mM/l). One millimole is, therefore, one one-thousandth of 90 grams of lactic acid dissolved in one litre of blood (1 mM/l). From the minute proportions it is obvious that this is a particularly potent liquid. At rest the normal blood lactate is roughly between 0.5 and 1.5 mM/l. Levels as high as 24 mM/l have been measured after maximum effort swims. It is also obvious that, for effective use, there is a need for a knowledge of basic physiology, and the practice of the basic training principles of adaptation, progressive overload and specificity. These have been covered in other chapters.

The testing involves taking blood samples which should be undertaken by **appropriately qualified** personnel. Written parental permission for all swimmers under the age of eighteen should be ensured before testing is done. The three metabolic processes have been described in chapter 3.

> "During exercise the blood lactate (lactic acid) level is the only reliable indicator of anaerobic metabolism and hence of the balance between aerobic energy utilisation." The *Analox Instruments* Ltd. information leaflet stating the value of lactate testing.

As the intensity (speed) of swimming increases, so the blood lactate level increases. At low levels of intensity there is a relatively low increase in lactate for a considerable increase in speed. The rate of increase continues in this manner until a point is reached at which the rate of lactate production exceeds the rate of disposal from the bloodstream. This metabolic balance point has been called the "anaerobic threshold", or "OBLA" (onset of blood lactate). After this state has been reached the position reverses and there is a great increase in lactate level for relatively small increases in speed. One of the aims of training is to attain the maximum speed possible before this point is reached, i.e., within the aerobic capacity. Lactic acid is one of the crucial factors in the inhibition of muscle action and fatigue. Fig. 5.3 on page 49 expresses as a graph typical lactate production as swimming speed increases.

There is a genetic limit to the amount of lactate an individual can produce. This can only be reached if the body is appropriately trained and motivated to swim at maximum intensity. This is known as the **Potential Peak Lactate.** At any given time the body can reach a maximum lactate level for its current state of training if the motivation is high enough to ensure maximum effort. This is called the **Peak Lactate,** but it may not be as high as the potential peak. For truly fast swimming the swimmer must be able to get as close as possible to the genetic limit.

> "The better the anaerobic capacity the higher the swimmer can raise his lactic acid value and the faster he can swim".

Dr. Ørjan Madsen, ASCA Clinic, 1986.

It does not follow, however, that the reverse is true, i.e., that to reach the potential maximum lactate level the swimmer must swim at the maximum potential speed. Maximum potential lactate could be reached

Figure 5.3 Profile of a swimmer whose training has been balanced over a three week training period

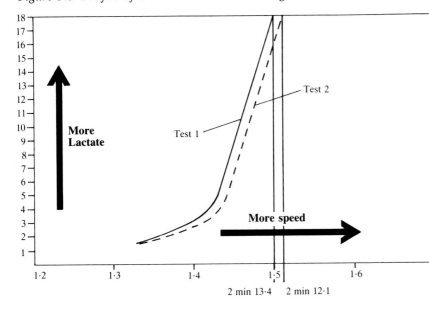

The movement of the graph is to the right and downward with the peak being maintained. There is an improvement of aerobic capacity whilst maintaining anaerobic power.

Figure 5.4(a) "No pain, no gain", philosphy

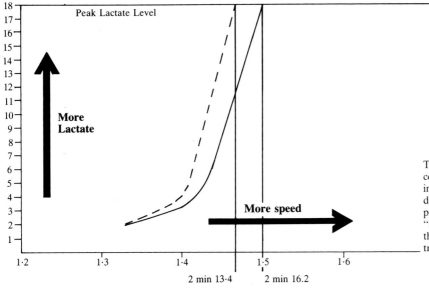

This Profile shows a swimmer who has concentrated on anaerobic power training working at maximum effort on distances of 50-200 metres with long passive rests. It is typical of many "sprinters". This frequently happens so that as competition approaches, aerobic training has been minimal.

Figure 5.4(b) Profile of a swimmer with no aerobic training

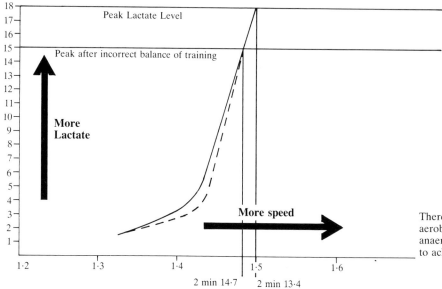

There has been a marked improvement in aerobic capacity but a regression in anaerobic power. The swimmer is unable to achieve peak lactate.

Figure 5.4(c) Profile of a swimmer on course for recovery

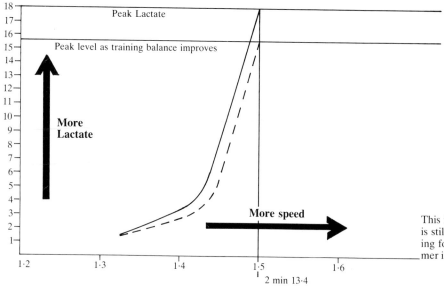

This is similar to Figure 5.4(b), but there is still insufficient anaerobic power training for improvement in time. This swimmer is back where he started 6 weeks ago!

simply by training always at maximum effort, a mistake which has often been made, but this would almost certainly mean **not** reaching maximum potential speed. Swimmers must develop **all** aspects of the energy systems in an appropriate balance to be able to achieve maximum performance. The graphs indicate how training imbalance reduces the chances of achieving maximum performance levels. Only lactate testing is a reliable indicator that the correct balance is being achieved (Fig. 5.4(a), 5.4(b), 5.4(c) on pages 49-50).

In studying these graphs the training principles must be remembered:
- Adaptation **always** occurs;
- It occurs **specifically,** i.e., only at the intensity of the exercise;
- The systems must be **overloaded** precisely and systematically for maximum beneficial adaptation to occur.

If the swimming stimulus is applied incorrectly, either by being too great (over training) or by being too low, then the efficiency of the system will regress.

The Tests

There are several types of tests, each designed for a specific purpose:
- Peak lactate test
- Current status/state assessment
  – Profiling
  – Two-swim test
- Random testing

Clearly, the collection of blood is an invasive process. The highest levels of hygiene must be maintained at all times. Only appropriately qualified people should undertake the collection of blood samples.

Method
Blood is collected in a small glass capillary tube containing anticoagulant and stabilisers. Specially treated capillary tubes are available which allows the blood to be stored over a period of days. It is possible, using a modified version of these capillary tubes, to have testing carried out by a postal service. A very small sample of this blood is then injected into the *Analox Analyser* and a result is printed out some twenty seconds later.

Peak Lactates Test
This test is undertaken as the result of a maximum effort performance, usually in competition. It has been stated that lactic acid diffuses into the bloodstream throughout the body and the time this takes differs from swimmer to swimmer. This diffusion and blood lactate increase continues after the cessation of exercise, so it is necessary to take samples at regular intervals, usually of one minute, for several minutes until the peak level is past. Initially, samples are taken for up to 11 minutes for very high level senior swimmers, but as the individual tendencies for peaking are noted the time span can be modified.

Current Status/State Assessment
Profiling – This is simply a method of obtaining an accurate graph or "profile" of the state of the energy systems, by testing the lactate levels after each of a series of test swims of increasing intensity. The more measurements there are included in the graph the more accurate will be the profile, and the more accurate will be the location of the anaerobic threshold. Profiling, however, is a long and expensive procedure to be undertaken in a club situation, as the example below shows. There are a number of methods, but the principle remains the same. The example is for a 200m specialist.

Example

The swimmer swims 8 × 200m as follows:

- 3 × 200m on 3 mins 30 secs at 88% of current best time;
- A blood sample is taken 1 min after the third 200m;
- 3 min rest after the third swim;
- 2 × 200m on 3 mins 30 secs at 90% of current best time with the blood sample taken after the second swim;
- 3 mins rest after second swim;
- 1 × 200m at 93% of current best time with blood sample taken after one minute, two minutes and three minutes;
- 5 mins rest;
- 1 × 200m 95% of current best time with blood sample taken as in previous test, or before and after usual peak time if longer than 3 mins;
- 20 mins rest;
- 1 × 200m maximum effort with the blood samples regularly taken up to 10 minutes (depending on knowledge of swimmer).

Figure 5.5 Anaerobic Lactic Acid training zones

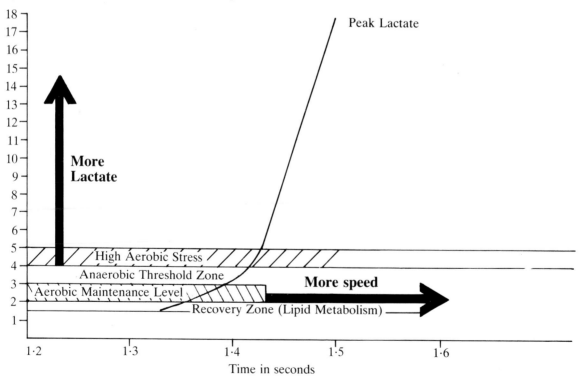

With careful organisation, and the support of knowledgeable and reliable personnel, this is not as daunting a task as it may seem. However, it undoubtedly makes serious demands on resources. The result of the profile is that all the intensities for training at various levels can be ascertained. It is then a matter of knowing the appropriate balance of training and methods of training to place the intensities into the training programme. Further profiling will show the **effect** of the training.

Ideally, this test should be undertaken every month, or even every three weeks, but the resources involved are usually far in excess of all but national teams. Fortunately, there are methods which cost much less and are just as effective. Fig. 5.5 on page 52 shows how the profile is "zoned" to indicate at what levels various types of training are most effective.

The Two-Swim Test – Much credit here must go to those specialists who have devised tests using massive banks of data accumulated over many years. The origin of these tests goes back to the former East German regime. In 1974, Dr. Alois Mader defected from East to West Germany taking with him both a massive amount of data and his considerable knowledge of the subject. At the *Deutschen Sporthoschule, Köln,* work proceeded to produce the forerunner of tests, the "Two-speed Test." This test utilised the lactate levels of two 400m swims, one at about anaerobic threshold level, and the other at maximum effort. With the use of the tables compiled from the data banks this provided a type of profile, and a standard reference point, from which training intensities could be planned. Unfortunately, this test also called for demands on a precious commodity, namely, time.

With this in mind, and with a desire for further accuracy, Dr R. Howat and Dr M. Robson devised a very accurate and easily operated test of two 200m swims, and accompanied this with a set of tables of training intensities extending through all aerobic levels and just beyond – the key area for training. After a warm up, 2 × 200m are swum with 30 secs rest between. The pace of the swims must be equal, even and below 3.5 mM/l. This is quite low. A guide for those with no previous testing background is about 85% of a personal best time; remember, this is a guide only. Blood is taken one minute after the second swim. From this test the current state of the aerobic system can be assessed and training times established using the tables developed by Doctors Howat and Robson.

Random Testing

This measures the validity of the assessment tests. It simply involves running tests on sets of swims planned from the use of the previously described "2 × 200" test. During these sets swimmers are brought out of the water and tested to ascertain that the lactate levels determined from the tables are actually being reached by the swimmer. For those fortunate enough to have the use of an *Analox Analyser* these tests can be run during a set. If necessary, modifications can be made immediately. Tests can also be undertaken by post, but this takes longer. The tables have been found to be remarkably accurate.

Children and Lactate Testing

Children are not merely miniature adults. They are different in many ways, one of which is the energy delivery systems. Children have little anaerobic capacity. Anaerobic glycolysis, and the production of lactic acid, develops during puberty. The body's systems develop at different rates and at different ages, so it is impossible to lay down any particular age at which lactate testing becomes viable. Psychologically, too, lactate testing is for the serious swimmer who has the understanding and the appreciation of long-term aims. It is not in the best interests of children to be seriously pressured before the age of about 14 years of age for girls, and 15/16 years of age for the boys. It might be physiologically interesting to trace the development, but this is no justification for including it in a swimming programme for young people.

Many teachers/coaches feel that lactate testing at "club" level is difficult and unnecessary. Some suggest that, since small clubs have limited time, lactate testing is inappropriate. Much depends on just how much the teacher/coach wishes to help the older swimmers. A lack of water time is an even greater reason for using tests since they offer accuracy of planning and permit the use of the limited time to the best advantage. Possession of an analyser is not necessary since a testing programme can now be undertaken by post. Seminars, courses and a mass of literature on basic physiology are available, and teachers/coaches owe it to their swimmers to learn about these methods of assessment.

Speed

The main objectives underpinning the swimming progress of children are:
- The development of the love of water, enjoyment and satisfaction;
- The development of technique;
- The development of basic speed;
- The development of the aerobic capacity;
- The development of understanding.

Most of these have been the subjects of other chapters and it will be obvious that they are compatible. Most people like to swim powerfully and fast, even if only for a very short distance. So the development of basic speed is fun, and this also applies to its testing.

Basic speed is the greatest speed a swimmer can achieve without any assistance, and without the interference of fatigue. It is tested by a time measurement of a maximum effort swim over a very short distance, i.e., unencumbered by fatigue, and with no influence of dive, push off or fixed finish.

Method

On the poolside, at fixed and measured distances appropriate to the age and ability of the swimmers to be tested, markers are placed. These distances can be from 5 metres, for the very young, to 15 metres for the top class, elite swimmer. **Each marker** consists of **two** uprights, set one behind the other, in line and at right angles to the poolside. When the two uprights are lined up by the eye of the observer any object passing this line will always do so in precisely the same spot. The problems of parallax, therefore, are avoided. Times are always taken as the swimmer's head reaches the line of sight.
- The swimmer to be tested sets off at sufficient distance from the first marker to permit maximum speed to be achieved before timing begins;
- The watch is started as the swimmer's head crosses the first marker;
- The watch stopped as the swimmer's head reaches the second marker;
- Swimmers must be told to swim several strokes past the marker;
- Three or five swims constitute a test. Extreme times are eliminated and either the fastest of the remainder, or an average of the remainder, is the time noted as the basic speed;
- The speed to be used is calculated by dividing the time by the distance;
- Recorders and timers are required;
- The swimmer should have the same timer on every occasion.

Apart from the markers, a stop watch and recording materials are the only other essentials

Speed of Starts, Turns and Finishes

- **Starts** – The test distances are:

  Standard   7.5 metres

  Children   6 metres (5 metres for Back Crawl)

  Breaststroke   8 metres to 12 metres depending upon the age and ability of the swimmer.

Method

- The poolside marker is placed at the appropriate distance from the start point;
- The timer, who is also the starter, sits in line with the marker and uses the correct starting procedure;
- The watch is started on the starting signal and stopped as the swimmer's head reaches the marker line;
- The time is called out to the recorder and the watch reset;
- False starts are ignored.

The administrative procedure is the same as for basic speed testing

- **Turns** – The test distances are:

  Standard   7.5 metres (2 metres and 5.5 metres)

  Children   6 metres (2 metres and 4 metres)

  Breaststroke   to 10 metres (2 metres and up to 8 metres)

Method

- One marker is placed 2 metres from the end of the pool. The second marker is placed the appropriate distance from the end of the pool, as suggested above by the numbers in brackets;
- The time is taken from the 2 metre mark and back to the further marker, i.e., the turn, the push off and the transition into stroke;
- The timer has to be alert enough to start the watch at 2 metre marker, then move quickly to be in position to stop the watch at the second marker;
- Again, timing is "head to head", and the swimmer must attain full speed before reaching the first marker and must maintain it through the second.

- **Finishes** – The test distance is 5 metres.
- The marker is placed 5 metres from the finish, and the watch is started as the swimmer's head crosses the marker line;
- The watch is stopped as the finish is made, hopefully not with the head!

- **Pacing** – Monitoring pacing is almost always undertaken during competition by taking race splits and stroke rates at strategic points during the race. These are used later in training. Another method is to plan what race pacing should be and use lactate testing for appropriate cumulative distances. This is very time consuming and is for the top, elite swimmer and coach working on a one-to-one basis.

Monitoring Guidelines

Efficiency, speed, accuracy relevance and communication are the secrets of successful monitoring. The British Association of Sports Sciences (BASS) contacted through the National Coaching Foundation, lays down excellent detailed guidelines for testing in many areas. However some simple guidelines may be helpful:

- The isolation of the feature(s) to be monitored is essential. It is pointless testing if the area to be tested is encumbered with other factors;

- The maintenance of safety at all times is essential;
- The reliance on swimmer judgement should be minimised;
- Activities should avoid complexity, e.g., swimmers should not be asked for exacting and precise pace control. "Swim maximum effort," is a simple instruction, easily understood;
- Efficient, accurate administration is vital;
- Tests should be organised so that they are completed within the attention span of the group;
- Swimmers must follow instructions and rules. Fooling about can ruin tests and waste both time and resources;
- Only accepted methods of testing should be employed (Refer to BASS);
- Tests are only of concern to the individual. Comparisons should only be with a swimmer's previous results. Individual differences are such that "league tables" and ranking lists serve no purpose. Inevitably, swimmers will make their own comparisons, but this must be played down by the teacher/coach;
- Results and findings are confidential. Swimmer privacy must be guarded at all times. Swimmer, and possibly parental agreement, should be obtained before any results are made public;
- Assuming such agreement is forthcoming, results should be made known as soon as is possible after the tests.

Chapter 6

Dry Land Training

Tony Holmyard

Introduction

Dry land training, or **land conditioning,** as it is sometimes called, is a broad term describing a variety of activities done out of the water in order to improve competitive swimming performance. It may be directed at flexibility, muscle fitness, cardio-vascular condition, or perhaps all three, and could involve:

- mobilising and stretching exercises;
- resistance work with barbells, dumbells, pulleys, elastic cords, machines, or the body's own weight;
- a variety of aerobic activities such as jogging, circuit-training or exercise to music.

It is a controversial subject which attracts widely differing views as to its degree of effectiveness and the best methods to be employed. However, dry land training is generally accepted as a valuable supplement to water work, but not as a substitute for it. Many teachers/coaches use it to provide variety in the training programme, particularly at times when water may not be available.

There is plenty of scientific evidence to show that exercising on land can perhaps improve flexibility of joints, strength and muscular endurance more effectively than in the water, simply because the resistance, or workload, can be more readily controlled and is not limited to that offered by the water. The evidence is less clear-cut as to whether all the gains made on land are transferred into swimming performance. Most research shows that transfer can be considerable, but depends a great deal on the specificity of the exercises. We need to design activities that exercise the same muscle groups, through the same range of movement and speeds of contraction, as those used in the swimming situation if we are to derive maximum benefit.

There is a concept of "Readiness" in child development which recommends that children should engage in activities appropriate to their various stages of physical, social or psychological development. To pursue activities prematurely puts them under some stress, takes a lot of the fun out of life and offers only very short-term gains. Other children, starting later, quickly catch them up. In their early years at a swimming club children like to play, be with their friends, learn new skills and have a little fun. We should not rob them of this period of light-hearted enjoyment which engenders a love of the sport and makes them much more likely to stay the course and develop into really good senior swimmers. Ideally, a swimmer's development is progressive over many years. The early years should concentrate on developing a wide range of swimming skills which become more specific and selective as maturity approaches. Similarly, with physical conditioning. Young people should pursue a broad spectrum of physical education activities which become more specific and demanding as they mature and discover where their talents really lie. Well-meaning, but ill-informed, adults often thrust children into serious physical conditioning programmes before they are able to benefit from them and they become disillusioned or bored. This applies very much to dry land training.

Only limited forms of dry land training should be introduced to swimmers before puberty. This could include flexibility work as this quality tends to deteriorate from about the age of ten years. It could also include moderate amounts of body weight exercises, sometimes called *Calisthenics,* as most children can safely handle their body weight without risk of injury. Heavy resistance work, such as weight-training, should not be offered to children until after puberty. Immature bones are very susceptible to damage, especially at the growth-plates (epiphyses), near the ends of the bone shafts, which are made up of soft cartilage-type material. As the child passes through puberty into adulthood the growth-plates ossify and fuse into the shaft to form a much stronger unit. Other areas of risk are at the points where tendons are attached to bones and these, too, can be damaged by application of extreme force, or repeated strong forces, even to the point of tearing the attachment away from the bone.

All children go through a similar process of maturation but, unfortunately, not at the same age. So it is not possible to put a simple recommendation of age for the safe commencement of heavy resistance training. Somewhere between 14 and 20 years of age bones stop growing and ossify. Both boys and girls can vary in their arrival at maturity by about two years either side of the average for their gender. As a rule girls will mature about two years before boys. As a rough guide 15 years for most girls, and 16 years for most boys, would be an acceptable time to start weight training, but a very watchful eye would have to be kept for late developers and their programme would need modifying accordingly. The strengthening of the skeleton comes about at the same time as the increased production of the male hormone *Testosterone,* which stimulates the growth of muscle in young men. To engage in strength training before this change in hormonal balance is largely unproductive (again the concept of "Readiness"). Young women secrete relatively small quantities of this hormone and, consequently, do not put on muscle bulk to the same degree. They can improve the quality of muscle fibre by exercise, but quantity is more difficult to acquire and many young women who might consider it unfeminine to develop muscle bulk will need reassurance on this point.

On the grounds of safety and effectiveness, therefore, heavy resistance exercises are not advised for swimmers until they are reaching the end of their adolescent growth spurt, and then it should be introduced progressively and with caution.

Flexibility

Flexibility is the freedom to move the body with a general absence of stiffness. It can be defined as the range of movement (ROM) about a joint or group of joints. **Static flexibility** refers to a ROM with no emphasis on speed, whereas **Dynamic flexibility** is the ability to use a ROM in performing an activity at normal or rapid speed.

Lack of flexibility can directly affect skill, a critical factor in swimming performance, by reducing the desired range of arm or leg movements or causing compensatory movements which interfere with streamlining. For instance, a Front Crawl swimmer with poor shoulder flexibility eithers enter the hand short of the ideal point, or achieves that point by lateral displacement of the shoulder and, or, the hips. The cross-section presented to the forward direction is increased and streamlining deteriorates. A Butterfly swimmer with stiff shoulders needs to heave the body higher out of the water to affect clean recovery of the arms than a swimmer with flexible shoulders. Breaststroke swimmers will obtain less effective traction if they cannot cock the feet fully outwards, (dorsiflexion and eversion), at the commencement of the backward kick. Nor will they fully utilise the "propeller effect" of the feet if their ankle joints have restricted ability to evert and invert, (turn on the inner and outer borders), which changes the pitch of the feet in the final thrust of leg action. Good flexibility also saves energy expenditure as it reduces the internal resistance of the muscles to movement during swimming.

However, in addition to maintaining or improving efficiency, flexibility work has a protective role to play. Thankfully, swimming injuries are few, but the vast majority of them are *overuse* problems involving damage and inflammation of the soft tissue of the body. Shoulders, knees and elbows are the commonest sites and these can be protected to some extent by maintaining good flexibility in the long term. In the short term, however, flexibility exercises should be incorporated into warm-up procedures, not only because a warmed and stretched muscle is less prone to injury, but also because it will contract more powerfully.

There are two main categories of flexibility work. They both work, but with advantages and disadvantages:

- **Ballistic stretching** – bouncing or jerking actions which take the limbs or body parts beyond their normal range. This should not be confused with mobilising or limbering-up movements which are often used in the first part of a warm-up, or as immediate pre-race activity, simply to lubricate the joints and get them moving smoothly within their normal range. Muscles contain stretch receptor nerves which are sensitive to sudden stretching which could tear muscle fibres. They create a reflex action which partially contracts the muscle in opposition to the sudden original stretch. This acts as a protective mechanism. Vigorous bouncing, or flinging movements, can over-ride the reflex action and force the muscle quickly beyond its normal length. It does stretch the muscle, but tends to cause tiny tears in the muscle fibres which result in soreness and stiffness the next day and can gradually accumulate small quantities of scar tissue, which is non-elastic, and gradually reduces the muscle's resilience. If Ballistic Stretching is used, it should be preceded by mobilising and static stretching to minimise these damaging effects;

- **Static stretching** – also effective and involves stretching and holding in the elongated position in two phases. This method is recommended because it is simple and the risk of damage is small.

  Phase 1 The muscle is stretched to its normal full extent, often called the point of discomfort. That position is held for about ten seconds, which allows the stretch reflex to subside and the muscle becomes more relaxed.

  Phase 2 The muscle is stretched further, elongating it beyond its habitual length and then held for a short period, about five seconds initially, then the length of the stretch is gradually built up. Conscious relaxation of the muscle allowing it to "give" will assist the process. This method is recommended because it is simple and safe, being controlled by the swimmer who is unlikely to stretch beyond the muscle's margin of elasticity.

Proprioceptive Neuromuscular Facilitation (PNF)

This is a relatively new, and more complex, approach to developing flexibility and can take a variety of forms. It requires a sound knowledge of the theory of muscle action. It is time consuming and carries more risk of injury than static stretching when an untrained partner is used to provide assistance. So with groups, particularly youthful, non-expert groups, **Static Stretching** is the safer option.

Any developmental stretching should be preceded by a thorough warm-up using mobilising exercises within the body's present range of movements and a variety of body body movements to raise the temperature. If the situation is cool, adequate, loose clothing should be worn to keep the body warm. Care should be taken not to force joints to exercise positions where bony surfaces grind together or nip cartilages, particularly in the spinal column. As in most forms of training, flexibility work should have a basis of general exercises with special areas of the body receiving additional attention according to the particular requirements of the individual and the swimming stroke favoured.

59

Examples of static stretching exercises for swimmers

Figure 6.1 Overhead stretch

Figure 6.2 One up, one down, shoulder extension

Overhead Stretch – these may be done either at home or on the poolside as part of the warm-up. Reach overhead, crossing the wrists so that the palms of the hands face each other and interlock. Extend the arms and shoulders vertically, keeping the spine flat as in a swimming push-off. (See Fig. 6.1)

One up, one down, shoulder extension – reach up with one arm and down with the other keeping them both close to the body line. Press both arms back. (See Fig. 6.2)

Figure 6.4 Back stretch

Figure 6.3 Shoulder girdle stretch

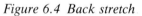

Shoulder girdle stretch – kneeling, place extended arms on the seat or back of a chair, press the chest and head downwards, keeping the arms straight. (Can also be done standing, bent at the hips with hands over any firm support). (See Fig. 6.3)

Back stretch – reach over the head with one arm and "walk" the fingers down the spine. With the free hand grasp the elbow and assist into the final stretch position. (See Fig. 6.4)

Figure 6.5 Back of shoulder stretch   *Figure 6.6 Front of shoulder stretch*

Back of shoulder stretch – reach across the front of the body beyond the opposite shoulder. Grasp the elbow with the free hand and assist into the final stretch position. (See Fig. 6.5)

Front of shoulder stretch – raise one arm sideways to the horizontal and fix the hand against the wall. Turn the body away from the hand stretching the muscles across the front of the shoulder and chest. (See Fig. 6.6)

Figure 6.7 Side to side stretch   *Figure 6.8 Chest stretch*

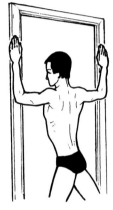

Side to side stretch – with feet comfortably apart, lean the head and the upper body to one side. Raise one arm over and beyond the head to assist the stretch. (Weight may be supported by the free hand on the hip). (See Fig. 6.7)

Chest stretch – standing in a doorway, raise the arms and bend the elbows at right angles to rest against door frame. Press the body forward (different parts of the shoulder and chest can be stretched by raising or lowering the hands). (See Fig. 6.8)

Figure 6.9 Thigh stretch

Thigh stretch – grasp the ankle and pull it to the buttocks, keeping the hip forward and the knee beneath the hip. Keep balance with the free hand against a wall or chair. (By grasping the toes, ankle extension can also be aided). (See Fig. 6.9)

Hamstring stretch – seated on the floor, legs apart, grasp one ankle and pull chest towards the thigh keeping the knee straight. The free leg may be bent. (This is safer for the spine than toe-touching in the standing position). (See Fig. 6.10)

Figure 6.10 Hamstring stretch

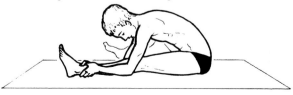

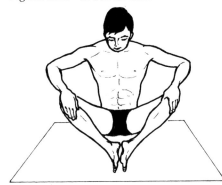

Figure 6.11 Groin stretch

Figure 6.12 Calf stretch

Groin stretch – seated on the floor with soles of the feet together and close into the buttocks, press the knees outwards and downwards with the hands. (See Fig. 6.11)

Calf stretch – take a large stride foward allowing the front knee to bend. Straighten the rear knee and squeeze the heel to the floor, keeping the rear foot facing straight ahead. (See Fig. 6.12)

Back of ankle stretch (Achilles Tendon) – place one foot forward a little in front of the other, then drop the weight down onto the rear foot, keeping the heel down and pushing the knee forward. (See Fig. 6.13)

Ankle extension (more correctly called "plantar flexion") – seated, grasp the toes and pull the ankle to an extended position. (Ankle may also be assisted in flexion, eversion and inversion, i.e., turning on its sides). (See Fig. 6.14)

Figure 6.14 Ankle extension

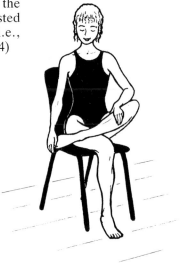

Figure 6.13 Back of ankle stretch

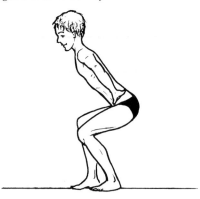

Figure 6.15 Ankle and knee stretch

Ankle and knee stretch – standing, grasp the foot and lift it close to the buttocks, pressing the foot forward and outward to stretch both ankle and knee joints. (See Fig. 6.15)

Muscle Fitness

Muscle fitness in swimming can be considered under three related headings. The development of any of these qualities is not done in isolation from the others:

- **Strength** – the ability to exert force. It is often measured as the maximum force that can be applied by a muscle or group of muscles in a single effort;
- **Power** – the product of strength and speed and is more important in sprint swimming than in the longer distance events. It is the application of strength at speed;
- **Muscular endurance** – the ability to repeat sub-maximal force many times over. It is a valuable quality in all swimming events but its importance increases with the distance to be raced.

Training can be geared to improve each of the qualities according to the particular demands of competition but, to a considerable extent, individuals will be suited to sprint events or to longer events according to the proportion of different types of muscle fibres they are born with. Without going into detail beyond the scope of this chapter, humans possess 3 types of muscle fibres: **Fast Twitch, Slow Twitch** and some **in between.** The Fast Twitch fibres contract quickly, produce great force but fatigue easily. The Slow Twitch fibres contract at slower speeds, are less powerful, more fatigue resistant and are suited to aerobic or endurance work. The function of the *In Betweens* will to some extent depend on the dominant type of training followed. Teachers/coaches generally agree that power (strength and speed) are vital in sprints of 100 metres or less, whilst muscular endurance is more critical in the longer events, with 200 metres being regarded as the dividing line for the training emphasis in dry land work.

Muscles can be exercised in a variety of different ways:

- **Isometric contractions** – used when tension is developed in a muscle, but it does not shorten its length. For example, a person seated at a very heavy table might place both hands under the table and attempt to lift it by flexing the elbows. No movement takes place but a static contraction occurs. Research shows that this type of action can increase strength, but the gain is limited to the particular angle of leverage used and does not apply to the rest of the range of movement of that joint. Hence, isometric exercise is of very limited use to swimmers who need to exert force through a very wide range of movement;

- **Isotonic contractions** – employed when a muscle creates tension and changes length, altering the distance between the two points of attachment to the bones. This is a familiar form of contraction to most people and the range of movement can easily be seen. A muscle contraction is isotonic when it is either shortening, i.e., acting concentrically, or lengthening, i.e., acting eccentrically. For example, getting up from a chair uses concentric action, sitting gently into a chair uses eccentric action. It might be assumed that by lifting free weights (barbells or dumbells) through similar movements to those used in swimming we would have an ideal training method for swimmers, but that is not the whole picture. It must be remembered that once we get a barbell moving, by overcoming its inertia and generating momentum, relatively little force is required to complete the movement. The mechanical advantage of levers also changes throughout a range of movement. Where there is poor leverage greater force is required from the muscle. Where leverage is good, less force is required. Also the muscle itself varies in its ability to create tension. This is due to the fact that the overlap between the microscopic fibres which produce muscular contraction is other than optimal at certain points throughout the range of contraction.

Manufacturers of training equipment have tried to compensate for these problems by designing weight-training equipment with oval shaped cams as pulley wheels and levers that offer changing mechanical advantage. They aim, with varying degrees of success, to keep the tension required of the muscle approximately the same throughout the movement.

- **Isokinetic exercise** – means literally, *same speed*. Like isotonic exercise, contractions may be concentric or eccentric in nature. Various types of apparatus have been designed to offer a resistance to movement that matches the force being applied by the muscles. These are known as *Isokinetic* machines. The *swim bench* is an example of this where the speed of muscle contraction is kept the same throughout the movement by presenting an equal, opposing resistance to the force being applied. These

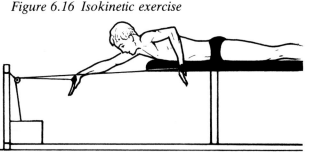

Figure 6.16 Isokinetic exercise

machines overcome most of the problems of training on land, as the same limb movements and speeds can be used as in the water, so the training effect is very specific. (See Fig. 6.16)

Training principles applied to dry land work

Several principles related to dry land training are worthy of note:

- **Adaptation** – muscles adapt to the stress of resistance training by the fibres growing thicker and by the capillaries supplying them increasing in number. But that is only part of the process. Neural changes also take place and the nerve pathways connecting the brain and spinal cord to the muscles become more efficient. The implication being that strength is latent within us, that many muscle fibres lie dormant, and we have to learn to use them through training;

● **Overload and progression** are linked – a muscle needs to be overloaded, or worked harder than the load normally encountered, if it is to improve its capabilities. After an initial gain in strength or muscular endurance, the original work load will not be sufficient to develop further growth, so the level has to be progressively increased over a period of time;

● **Reversibility** – this is adaptation in reverse. Gains made are not permanent and will deteriorate if training ceases, i.e., the body will adapt to the level demanded of it. Hard work is required to increase muscular strength or endurance, but less work is needed to maintain a particular level once it has been reached. This indicates that complete, prolonged breaks from training are inadvisable. Swimmers do need breaks to retain psychological freshness, but the breaks should be short or incorporate a moderate level of training as a maintenance programme;

● **Specificity** – general training is a good pre-requisite for specific training, whether it be water-work or dry land work. It prepares the body generally for more intense stresses to follow and, also, recognises the fact that we have other functions as human beings beside swimming in races; no reputable coach would like to see swimmers develop unbalanced physiques. However, specific training is the most effective form. A great deal of time has been wasted in the past developing forms of strength and muscular endurance that have not been directly related to competitive swimming. Research shows increasingly that swimmers need to exercise the same muscle groups, through the same ranges of movement, and at the same speeds as used in competition, to gain the best training effects. It is not just a case of physical adaptation, but also involves neural pathway efficiency, too. Swim benches, probably give the best transfer of training from land work to water-work.

Safety

1. All equipment should be well maintained.
2. If free weights are to be used they must be securely attached to the bar and checked at each use. Bars should be stripped down and both bars and weights stored correctly after use.
3. The working space should be clear of all obstructions, protrusions and should be clean and dry.
4. Sensible footwear should be used to give a good grip and support the ankle. (no bare feet).
5. Trained supervisors should be used until the participants are well-versed in safety procedures and skilled movements.
6. Light loads should be used initially until skilled movements have been learned. Progress to heavier loads should be made gradually.
7. Work loads should be selected to suit the individual according to maturity, physique and experience. Comparisons between individuals should be avoided.
8. Breath holding during heavy resistance exercises should be avoided as this causes pressure within the chest. (A rapid rise in blood pressure occurs causing the blood flow back to the heart to be restricted. This is followed by a sudden drop in blood pressure accompanied by faintness or even black out).
9. Exercise that may damage the joints, such as excessive flexion or extension should be avoided. The spine and knee are common sites of injury during dry land training. Injuries are mostly the result of low concentration or lack of skill.
10. Use a safe format for every exercise session:

- **Warm-up** – consisting of light ballistic movements within the body's normal range of movement to mobilise the joints, and a variety of aerobic exercises such as jogging, skipping or light calisthenics at gradually increasing intensities. This should raise the heart rate and body temperature;

- **Stretching exercises** – covering all the main muscle groups of the body, and particularly those to be involved in heavy resistance work. Warm clothing should be worn up to this point and throughout the session if the air temperature is low;

- **Heavy resistance work** – the type most suitable to the individual, bearing in mind age and experience. If necessary, incorporate further warm-up and stretching of the particular muscle group to be exercised if the body starts to cool down;

- **Wind-down** – similar to the warm-up but in reverse, where the intensity of working is progressively reduced, so that the body returns to its normal state gradually. This, too, should include some light stretch exercises. This will assist the blood flow back to the heart and so disperse the waste products of exercise more widely. Recovery from exercise is quicker this way, and it also avoids subsequent stiffness due to accumulation of waste products in muscles that have been subjected to heavy workload.

Examples of Calisthenics or Body Weight Exercises, for muscular endurance.
These exercises require no apparatus and could be done either at home or on the poolside as part of the warm-up (Do as many repetitions as possible in 30 seconds on each exercise).

Figure 6.17 Press (push) ups

Press (Push) ups (Arms and shoulder) – from the front support position with back and legs straight, lower the chest to the floor then push up until arms are fully extended. (See Fig. 6.17)

Figure 6.18 Modified press ups

Modified press up – for those unable to manage full press ups, start from a kneeling position and proceed as above. (See Fig. 6.18)

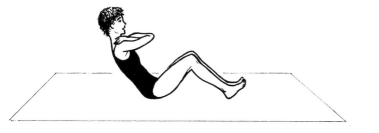

Figure 6.19 Bent knee sit ups

Bent knee sit ups – from back lying with knees bent and arms crossed to place hands on opposite shoulders, sit up to touch the knees with the elbows. A twist may be added touching the right knee with the left elbow, and vice versa (Bending the knees reduces the effect of the hip flexors and emphasises the action of the abdominal muscles). (See Fig. 6.19)

Figure 6.20 "Crunches"

"Crunches" (Abdominal) – as above, but with knees raised at about a right angle (This further isolates the hip flexors). (See Fig. 6.20)

Arm and leg raises (Back) – from the prone position, with arms extended beyond the head, raise right arm and left leg simultaneously, and vice versa (Do not over arch the spine). (See Fig. 6.21)

Leaping half squats (Legs) – from a half-squat position (knees at about a right angle), leap as high as possible, extending the legs to the tip of the toes, as in a racing start or push-off. (See Fig. 6.22)

Figure 6.21 Arm and leg raises

Figure 6.22 Leaping half squats

Back extension (Back) – in the prone position, clasp hands behind the back, then thrust hands towards the feet, squaring the shoulders (Do not over arch the spine). (See Fig. 6.23)

Figure 6.23 Back extension

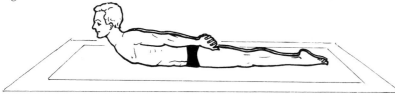

Chair dips (Arms) – from the sitting position, stretch the feet forward then slide the buttocks forward off the chair grasping the sides of the chair for support. Dip the body towards the floor, then raise it by extending the elbows and upper arms. (See Fig. 6.24)

Burpee (General) – from standing, drop down to place the hands on the floor shoulder width apart just in front of the feet. Shoot the legs out to the rear. Jump them in again, then stand up. (See Fig. 6.25)

Figure 6.25 Burpee

Figure 6.24 Chair dips

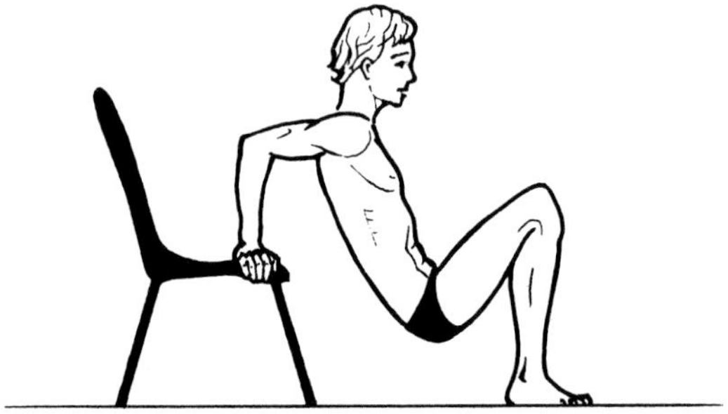

Examples of General Weight Training Exercises:
- to develop strength use heavy resistance with few repetitions;
- to develop muscular endurance use light resistance with many repetitions.

A reasonable compromise would be to select a resistance that would cause fatigue using 10 repetitions (referred to as a 10 RM, or 10 Repetition Maximum).

Figure 6.26 Bench press

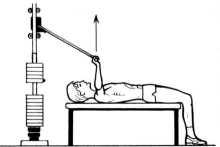

Figure 6.27 Wrist roller

Bench press – in the supine position on a bench with head and hips supported. Feet may be on the bench, or on the floor beneath the knees. The bar or machine handles are grasped at shoulder width, with shoulder directly beneath the hands. Bar is driven vertically upwards, exhaling. Inhale as the weight is lowered and the chest naturally expands. (See Fig. 6.26)

Wrist roller (Wrist flexors) – the weight is raised by rolling the attached cord round the bar, by alternately flexing the wrists. (See Fig. 6.27)

Leg extension (Thighs and calf) – adjust distance from the platform so that the knees are bent at right angles. Straighten the knees, using the thighs (quadriceps), then point the toes using the calf muscles, (As in a racing dive or push-off). (See Fig. 6.28)

Pull down to neck (Latissimus dorsi) – grasp the bar wider than shoulder width and pull it down as far as possible behind the neck. (See Fig. 6.29)

Knee extension (Thighs) – sitting with the knee joint directly over the end of bench, straighten the knee from the bent position. (See Fig. 6.30)

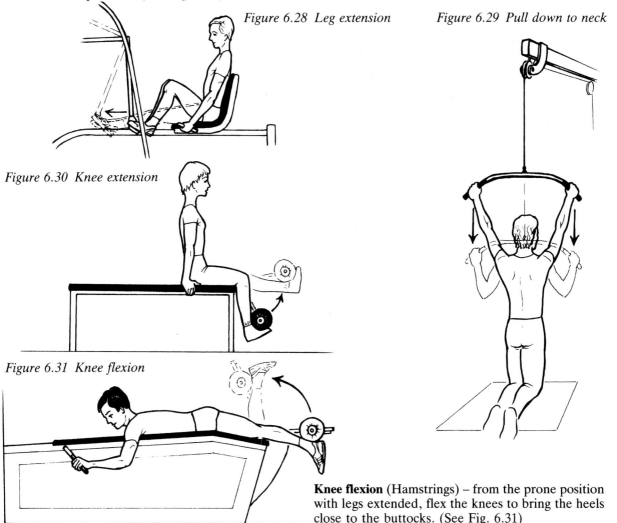

Figure 6.28 Leg extension

Figure 6.29 Pull down to neck

Figure 6.30 Knee extension

Figure 6.31 Knee flexion

Knee flexion (Hamstrings) – from the prone position with legs extended, flex the knees to bring the heels close to the buttocks. (See Fig. 6.31)

Press towards chest (Pectoralis) – with upper arms extended sideways, squeeze the arms together in front of the face. (See Fig. 6.32)

Overhead press (Shoulders and triceps) – seated directly beneath the bar, press from shoulder level to fully extend the arms above the head (Keep the spine straight). (See Fig. 6.33)

Forearm curl (Biceps) – grasping the bar at shoulder width with straight arms, flex the elbows through the fullest possible range of movement. (See Fig. 6.34)

Figure 6.32 Press towards chest   *Figure 6.33 Overhead press.*   *Figure 6.34 Forearm curl*

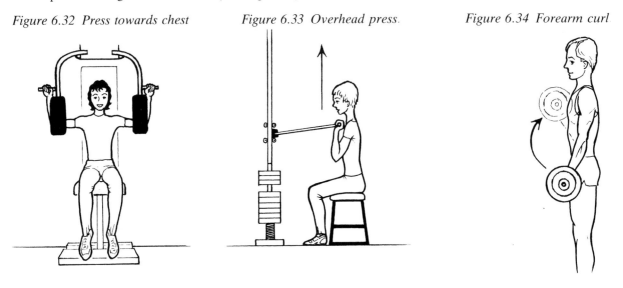

Examples of Swim-Specific Work

These should follow the swimming stroke pattern as closely as possible, using the same speed of movement. Build up the repetitions, using light load, to the same number of strokes used over the race distance. Then increase the load and build up the repetitions again.

Resistance of elastic cords can be progressively increased by shortening the elastic, by increasing the number of strands or by using thicker stronger cords.

Summary

Present research and empirical evidence concerning **dry land training** would suggest a long term approach from childhood to adulthood along the following lines:

- **Pre-pubertal ages** – flexibility exercises continuing throughout competitive swimming and beyond;
- **Pre-pubertal ages** – calisthenics using body weight as resistance in a general and balanced manner;
- **At puberty** – a weight training programme programme using light resistances in a general and balanced manner, emphasising skill and safety;
- **Post puberty** – a general weight training programme using heavier resistances to develop strength;
- **Post puberty to adulthood**

– more specific weight training for power, (speed and strength), for sprinters, or muscular endurance for distance swimmers;
– isokinetic swim bench work using stroke specific movement patterns and speeds.

Figure 6.35 Breaststroke swimmer using a swim-bench

Figure 6.36 Front Crawl swimmer using stretch cords

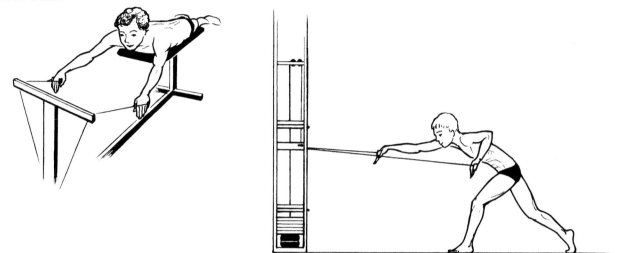

PART III

PROGRAMMING

Introduction to Part III

The whole essence of good teaching/coaching is not only knowing **what** to do but, also, knowing **how to plan its implementation.** The short and long term implications of training schedules, and their place in the competitive programme, is an example of long term planning. In addition the planning of sessions for the improvement of technique, or the introduction of new skills, all require considerable understanding of both the mental and physiological aspects of a swimmer's development. Part III suggests ways of approaching the task of planning work by offering both principles and examples of sound practices.

Chapter 7

The Teaching and Coaching of Children
Dr Colin Hardy

Introduction

Teaching is a generic term and it designates a family of activities of which training (coaching) and instruction are important members. In the present context it is assumed that training may often involve instruction, i.e., giving information in the form of directions, reasons and evidence and, in this sense, it is a type of teaching. However, whether the participants are performing endurance sets in a club environment or learning routine swimming skills in a school setting, the teaching of such activities requires the participants to understand what they are doing and why, and to be intelligent and reflective in the execution of them.

The teaching section in the *Level 1* publication in this series, focused on the planning and structure of lessons, evaluation procedures and teacher/coach functions during activity. This chapter will focus on leadership styles, technical skills of teaching and coaching, and the possible effects on the swimmers.

Leadership

Teachers/coaches of swimming are dealing with developing children. It is their job to influence the young swimmers in directions that are regarded as educationally desirable. However, as the adults who hold these positions do have a considerable amount of power and authority, it is important that they understand the type of effects their leadership styles might have on swimmers.

Authoritarian teachers/coaches tend to rely on whole-class activities, and swimmers either try to conform to a structure that is often based on a few talented swimmers or they lose interest and drop out. Teachers/ coaches who use a more democratic style pláce a greater emphasis on small groups and individuals working independently but, to be effective, this does require a positive act on their part to train the swimmers in self-direction and in the art of when and how to seek help. In any class or squad situation it is unlikely that the instruction is entirely whole-class or small-group or individualized, as teachers/coaches need to be flexible and to be able to adapt to the demands of the teaching-learning process. Therefore, teachers/ coaches must not only just engage swimmers in practices, but they must pay attention to swimmers' responses to their leadership styles and organizations, evaluate such responses and be prepared to make adjustments to their styles if necessary.

Management

In order to manage swimming settings effectively teachers/coaches must play a central role in defining expected swimmer behaviours. Therefore, they must have a clear idea of what behaviours are and are not appropriate in advance of any instruction. Swimmers need to know what to do when they first enter the pool. Does the teacher normally speak to the pupils prior to their entering the pool? Are the squad swimmers expected to assemble in their lanes, and to carry out a set warm up? By establishing such procedures teachers/coaches are able to start their sessions with the minimal amount of delay.

Figure 7.1 Some considerations for teachers/coaches about their leadership styles

Question	Considerations
1. Is your leadership style repressive?	Are you: making all the decisions? controlling all phases of the session? expecting conformity from all swimmers? discouraging swimmers from asking questions?
2. Do all the swimmers have a more or less equal chance to be successful?	Are you: giving the swimmers practices appropriate to their ability? catering for the different age and sex groups? considering the stroke strengths of the swimmers? expecting too much from some swimmers?
3. Are the swimmers being given the opportunities to learn to handle responsibility?	Do you expect the swimmers: to take responsibility for carrying out their tasks correctly? to be able to adapt your sessions? to share in the decision-making processes? to reflect on their experiences?
4. Do you have sufficient authority?	Are you: finding the swimmers hard to control? allowing the swimmers to make decisions without the relevant knowledge? allowing the swimmers to take over the leadership? finding it difficult to manage small groups?

Expected swimmer behaviour includes listening attentively during whole class activities. The pool is a noisy environment and any murmuring, talking or splashing by swimmers can lead to instructions not being heard. In addition, it is also a sound practice for teachers/coaches to have some technique for dealing with swimmers' questions and responses to questions, e.g., swimmer raises the hand.

It is common practice in swimming sessions for teachers/coaches to divide swimmers into several groups. With such a format are group leaders appointed to ensure that the tasks are carried out correctly? What is the procedure if swimmers in an unsupervised group need to check something with the teacher/coach? Can they interrupt if the teacher/coach is dealing with another group? Are the swimmers allowed to make adjustments until teacher/coach makes contact with them? Teachers/coaches must have some system covering such events otherwise swimmers may go off task, or even interfere with the deliberations of teacher/coach and other groups. Frequently equipment has to be shared among swimmers and teachers/ coaches must decide how such use will occur. For instance, teachers/coaches may decide that the kickboards are to be used by only two groups at any one time, or that starting blocks will be used by some of the swimmers while others practise turns at the other end of the pool.

Movement of swimmers from one part of the pool to another, dealing with the swimmers' personal needs and the end-of-session arrangements are other areas of swimming pool behaviour that need to be considered. Effective classroom management encompasses all these points.

Behaviour

Swimmers' attention

There are many reasons why swimmers are not attentive when tasks are communicated to them and, although teachers/coaches may not have control over some of these conditions, much of the inattention may be prevented. Teachers/coaches should not try to compete with a group of talkative swimmers, but they should wait until the swimmers have responded with quietness and attention to the given signal. If other activities in the pool are distracting the swimmers then bringing them closer in and, if possible, facing them away from the distraction will assist in control. With mixed age groups it is important that the older swimmers are dealt with in a more adult manner, i.e., request, rather than order, them to listen, and that their responses will set a norm for the younger members of the group.

At times swimmers become inattentive because they cannot hear the instructions or because they cannot see the demonstration properly. In order to overcome such problems teachers/coaches should continually evaluate the effectiveness of their communication, i.e., ask the swimmers, or other teachers/coaches, to comment on their effectiveness, and they should always look for a poolside position where they can be heard and seen by all swimmers (Hardy C.A. (1987), *Handbook for the Teacher of Swimming,* Pelham Books Ltd.). However, instructions and demonstrations should be as brief, concise and as accurate as possible, as young swimmers in particular, with their short attention span, may soon become inattentive. Although older swimmers may sometimes expect a fuller explanation about the task in hand, avoid delaying the on-task behaviour for any length of time, and supplement information during any breaks in the activities.

Behaviour problems

A swimmer who interferes with others swimmers, disrupts the activity or conflicts with the rules and expectation of the teacher/coach may be said to be causing problems. However, as many behaviour problems can be associated with a variety of factors related to the pupil and the teacher/coach, e.g., personality and socio-economic status of the pupil, lack of preparation of the teacher/coach, reaction to behaviour problems must be considered carefully. Also, teachers/coaches must be aware of the ownership of the problem. For example:

- did the swimmer's behaviour cause the teacher/coach to be annoyed?
  (teacher-owned problem)
- did the swimmers feel frustrated by events or by people other than the teacher/coach?
  (pupil-owned problem)
- are the teacher/coach and the swimmer frustrating each other's needs and goals?
  (shared problem)

Before reacting to a particular behaviour problem teachers/coaches will need to assess the importance of the following points:

- the frequency and length of the behaviour episode;
- the intensity of the behaviour and its effect on the swimmer's own activities, and its effect on other swimmers;
- the frequency of the behaviour with the swimmer's particular age group;
- the reasonableness of the behaviour given the circumstances.

Figure 7.2 Some considerations for teachers/coaches in reacting to swimmers' behaviour problems

Situation	Considerations
1. Swimmer is continually annoying the teacher/coach by being late for the session (teacher-owned problem)	Does the swimmer have transport difficulties? Does the swimmer deliberately hang around in the changing room and turn up late to annoy the teacher/coach?
2. Swimmer is frustrated by the derogatory comments of some spectators (pupil-owned problem)	Is the swimmer being over-sensitive to typical teenage banter? Do the comments reflect a more underlying problem of the swimmer's relationships with other club members?
3. Swimmer and teacher/coach angrily disagree over the relevance of the schedule? (shared problem)	Is the teacher/coach making a positive effort to explain the reasoning behind his selection? Can the teacher/coach see the swimmer's point of view? Is there a compromise solution?

Reactions to behaviour problems

Teachers/coaches should:

- be clear and firm in their reprimands, indicate clearly the swimmer who is being reprimanded, and emphasize the behaviour expected,
  "J...– you will **place** the float on the pool side"
- avoid being threatening,
  "J...– you will lose your place in the squad if you keep splashing the other swimmers"
- avoid harsh and emotional reprimands,
  "J..., leave the pool immediately" (anger is shown by the teacher/coach)

The timely reprimand can have an effect on others even though the reprimand was aimed at one person, i.e., ripple effect. Also, if teachers/coaches use simple reminders to swimmers as to the expected behaviours in the pool and encourage self-control among them, the unacceptable behaviour is less likely.

Communication

A critical aspect of swimming task presentation is selecting an effective means of communication. Based on the swimmers' characteristics and the content of the session, teachers/coaches may present a task verbally or physically, e.g., demonstration, or using both techniques, and they may supplement the presentation with other media materials, e.g., pictures. Once the task is clearly presented teachers/coaches will use verbal and physical cues, silence and non-verbal cues, questions, feedback and praise, to reinforce swimmer involvement.

Verbal communication

Clarity of instruction is an essential aspect of verbal communication. Teachers/coaches must not assume too much understanding on the part of the swimmer, and they should consider the ages and different learning characteristics of their swimmers. It must be remembered that young swimmers may not have the experience of older swimmers to bring to a new skill, and that their verbal skills are less advanced. For example, in trying to improve a younger inexperienced swimmer's Back Crawl arm pull the teacher/coach might be better to talk about the arm bending and straightening, and to accompany the instruction with a demonstration; with the more experienced, older swimmer the technicalities of the upward and downward sweeps might be more appropriate. However, the situation is not always as simple as this as a younger swimmer could be more experienced, and at a more advanced level, than the older swimmer.

Teachers/coaches must not only take into consideration the ages and levels of ability of the swimmers, but they must look at the type of content that is being presented. In swimming the skills are mainly closed (skills are often classified on a continuum ranging from "closed" through to "open". The greater the number of variables, e.g., players, environmental factors etc, involved in the skill, the closer to the "open" end of the continuum it becomes, e.g., a team game played in the open air) and teachers/coaches tend to create visual images of the critical elements of the skill, e.g., Breaststroke kick: "describe a circle with the feet". There are conditions in the teaching and coaching of swimming where the content can be classified as an open skill and, in such situations, teachers/coaches must give the kind of verbal cue that focuses on swimmers' adjusting their responses to meet changes in the environment. The cues needed for an emergency in water may include:

- think before you act;
- assess your own ability;
- assess the factors affecting the emergency;
- develop a plan of action;
- act quickly and decisively ensuring your own safety.

Even such skills as swimming turns can be labelled open skills, although their application is less complex than the lifesaving skills. With the Back Crawl "tumble" turn, for example, the swimmer may have to make refinements in the final approach to the wall and adapt the tightness of the tuck to maintain momentum. Cues for the refinement of response may include "spot the wall before tumbling", or "tuck tighter if too close".

Demonstration

In swimming visual communication often takes the form of a demonstration and it is frequently used with verbal explanations. The demonstration should be accurate, provide information, offer guidance and develop the swimmer's understanding (Fig. 7.3).

Figure 7.3 Guidelines for demonstration

	Advice to teacher/coach
● accuracy of movement	Check your demonstration in a mirror
● accuracy of position	If you are showing an arm action, bend at the waist and keep the trunk horizontal
● guidance to observations	Highlight the important aspects of the movement and visually 'freeze' the movement at critical points
● information	Explain why the skill should be performed in a particular way
● understanding	Check that the swimmers understand the movement and what they are expected to do

Swimmers can demonstrate movements more efficiently in water so teachers/coaches should look for swimmers who can demonstrate movements that can be clearly observed from the poolside.

Silence and non-verbal cues

Sometimes talk can be reduced by encouraging teachers/coaches to use pauses, facial expressions, body movements and gestures. A pause during a verbal instruction could be used to observe the swimmers' responses to instruction, or it could be a way of waiting for the class to stop talking and pay attention. A smile and a nod could suggest satisfaction with a swimmer's performance; a body and limb movement could re-emphasize the technique to be attempted; gestures could be used for stopping or starting swimmers or showing some emotion such as delight. However, the importance of acquiring such skills is that the teacher/coach develops a greater depth of possible technical effectiveness.

Questioning (soliciting) and responding

Questioning is a move made predominantly by teachers/coaches rather than by swimmers, and it is a technique to elicit verbal and non-verbal behaviours from swimmers, e.g., teacher/coach solicits, "Why do you think a horizontal body position is necessary for swimming? Swimmer responds, "It gives less resistance". If the answer is correct the teacher/coach may indicate with a nod or a brief verbal comment, but if the answer is incorrect or only partly right, the reaction of the teacher/coach may be to ask the question again or ask it in a different way. Teachers/coaches will find that once they have drawn swimmers' attention to an aspect of swimming, e.g., "Let's look at the body position in swimming", or "Let's look at the importance of warm-up", soliciting, responding, and reacting behaviours are all part of the interactive process between teachers/coaches and their swimmers.

Praise

Praise is often related positively to achievement, but it is important that it is used systematically in support of the attainment of swimming objectives by the swimmers. Praise commends the worth of, or expresses approval or admiration for swimmer behaviour, and it suggests a more intense response to the behaviour than such terms as 'feedback' or 'affirmation of correct response' (see *Level 1* publication in this series). The quality of teacher/coach praise depends upon it being used with contingency, specificity and sincerity. The praise must be contingent on performance of the behaviour to be reinforced, the praise should specify the particulars of the behaviour being reinforced and the praise should be sincere, e.g., the swimmer is praised ("well done") for completing the sets at the pace and time intervals requested. The tone of voice and smile of the coach indicates the sincerity of the praise.

On occasions praise can be effective when used in a more spontaneous and less systematic way. For example, an unexpected good performance by a swimmer may result in a teacher/coach expressing surprise and admiration for the performance. Sometimes teachers/coaches praise weak swimmers for their efforts rather than their achievements; in this sense praise is used as a form of encouragement. Swimmers' responses to praise may be varied and teachers/coaches must not assume that all praise is effective. It is possible that praise is more effective with the younger swimmers, as praise constitutes guidance from an authority figure. Once this concern for pleasing adults recedes in favour of peer orientation and other motives, praise may become a weak reinforcer. However, most swimmers like to be singled out and praised at times, as, indeed, do most human beings, and it is the task of teachers/coaches to monitor the responses of their swimmers to such treatment.

Figure 7.4 Guidelines for effective praise

Deliver systematically		Specify details of the achievement			Show sincerity
Focuses the swimmer's attention on the behaviour	**S**	**QUALITY**	**T**		Reward attainment
	W		**E**	**C**	
Helps the swimmer appreciate and place value on the performance	**I**	**EFFECTIVE**	**A**	**O**	Provide information about the value of attainment
	M	**PRAISE**	**C**	**A**	
	M		**H**	**C**	
	E		**E**	**H**	
Fosters intrinsic interest about swimming	**R**	**IMPLICATION**	**R**		Use past performances as a context for the present attainment
Only given in recognition of noteworthy effort or success at a difficult task		Implies that similar successes can be expected			(Adapted from Brophy, (1981), *Teacher praise: a function analysis* Review of Educational Research, 51 (1), 5-32).

Summary

By trying to understand the effects of leadership styles and the technical skills of teaching/coaching, it is hoped that teachers/coaches will adopt a more analytic and reflective approach to their work. Although there are dangers of dehumanization and prescriptiveness associated with the areas studied, if it helps to extend the teachers/coaches behavioural repertoire and increases their professional awareness the task has been worthwhile.

Chapter 8

Planning

Charlie Wilson

Introduction

The need for planning arises the moment there is a desire to achieve, e.g., "I should like to be..." or "I shall do...". The reasons for this motivation are many and varied; the desire burns strongly for some but for most it tends to be more superficial. For top athletes the ferocity of this motivation is very strong, and, often, it can be seen at an early age and determines their ambitions and goals. It is the task of teachers/ coaches and parents to guide and foster these ambitions with enthusiasm, not force. The enthusiasm should be tempered by experience, knowledge and care. When this happens it becomes "planning".

Many believe that, in spite of outside pressures to the contrary, genetics, natural instincts and talent will shine through. It is a comfortable thought, but, unfortunately, reality differs. The world is full of "If only" people, the sporting misplaced, whose natural abilities were never fulfilled. The reasons for missing out may be varied, but it is certain that a lack of sound planning is high on the list.

Planning, then, is of the utmost importance; there is truth in saying, "To fail to plan is to plan to fail".

Children and Planning

Planning for children, i.e., age group swimmers, follows all the basic principles outlined in Fig. 8.1, but there are essential differences which must be observed. In the natural order of things there is, from the time of birth, a gradual movement toward independence and freedom of choice. Initially, the authority is parental then, later, school. Additionally, swimming teachers/coaches become part of the scene. This carries a considerable burden of planning responsibility on those in authority. They should have:

- an understanding of the growth and development of children;
- empathy with and love of children.

Preparing means caring – caring means preparing

It must be remembered that children are not merely miniature adults; they are quite different, and one of the differences which influences planning is the child's concept of time. It is difficult for adults to cast their minds back to the time when next week's birthday was an age away – they seem to come so quickly as one gets older! The passage of time assumes a totally different meaning to an adult because less and less of it is left. This difference can be an obvious problem area when adults have the responsibility of planning for children. Planning in any detail for children should be short term – for a day or a week perhaps. The longer the time period, the less will be the plan's significance and motivating influence. Long term planning for children should be in loose, general terms and discussed, preferably, at the child's instigation. Constant nagging references to plans are likely to cause the child to lose interest in them.

So much talent is lost by overbearing planning, by the feeling of being trapped by pressures imposed by parents, teachers/coaches and often, too, by the attentions of the media hunting irresponsibly for the sensational appeal of the child prodigy or future star. Plans for children should follow natural physical growth and development. Reference was made above to the natural and progressive movement away from adult control. It is important that the teacher/coach should include in long term planning a steady move toward swimmer independence. The teacher/coach should learn to move away from the authoritarian approach to the consultative. The sequence over the formative years is:

- this is what you must do – authoritarian;
- this is what you should be doing;
- what do you think you should be doing? – consultative.

Moving through this sequence is one of the most difficult planning tasks for a teacher/coach to undertake.

As children grow older, and commitments and responsibilities increase, so much still remains outside their control, e.g., from genetic and health problems, through certain major commitments such as school attendance, right down to a simple, but very real problem of transport to the pool. Laying down rigid plans and rules without a sympathetic understanding of these outside influences can place great mental stress on a youngster, and is a certain pathway leading from love of the sport to a dislike of it and finally to "drop out". Teachers/coaches must then be aware of the problems likely to arise in their particular environment and plan accordingly. The approach should be to tackle the problems at source and not through the child and in forgetting this the teacher/coach obsession can often double a difficulty. It is true that teachers/coaches should be obsessive, but that obsession should be under control so that only enthusiasm is communicated. Making team rules which concern, for example, school or parents, without the appropriate consultation should be avoided.

Knowledge and understanding

The development of knowledge and understanding are also important aspects of planning, particularly if children are to be led toward self-reliance. There is far more to becoming a top swimmer than just swimming. The teacher/coach should also be an educator and there must be space and time in the plans for such things as the behavioural aspects of sport. "Sportsmanship", the development of a healthy life style and the inculcation of sound habits, should be written into plans and not just included as an afterthought. Consideration should be given:

- to when and how children learn to behave before, during and after competition;
- to how they learn about the necessity for the correct rest or the correct diet;
- to how and when they are taught about the personal disciplines in sport, e.g., punctuality, attendance and commitment? These are as important at the planning stage as the timing of the next major competition;
- to how motivation is initiated. Do the plans include methods of motivation from within? Intrinsic, or self motivation, is as important a matter to consider as external rewards and influences, (extrinsic motivation).

Human beings are most impressionable and vulnerable when they are young. Teachers/coaches are in an important and privileged position and it is important, therefore, that planning for children must be undertaken thoroughly and with great care.

Planning – General Principles

The planning of any course of action in life demands a logical application of principles. Planning for teaching/coaching is not exempt from this process (see Fig. 8.1).

Figure 8.1 Planning – Long term

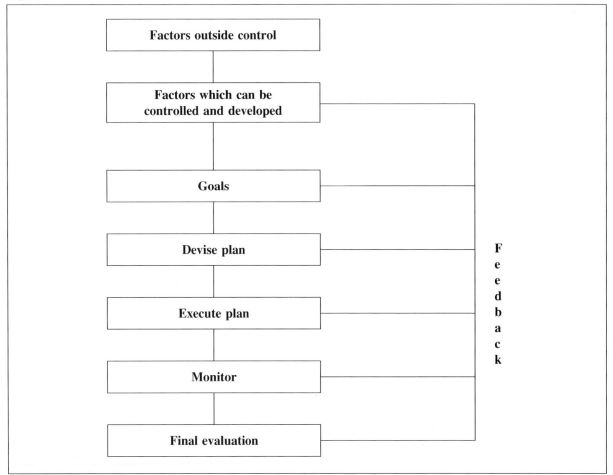

Factors outside control

The first heading in Fig. 8.1, namely, "Factors Outside Control", often causes difficulties for teachers/coaches because of their previously mentioned obsession and enthusiasm. They are also the eternal optimists and, thus, they are disinclined to take due regard to factors outside their control. Careful assessment of what is "beyond control" is vital, although there still ought to be a place for determination in their work. An insurmountable problem for one may be a challenge for another. It is a fine trait to see problems as challenges, but reality must also play its part. Exuberance without care, leading to a disregard of important control factors, often results in totally inappropriate plans, schedules and competitions being put in place.

Some important factors in this category are:

Geography (climate, terrain or communication)

There is some difference between a foggy January morning in a northern industrial city, with its ancient 33 yard pool, and the climate, on the same date, in affluent Southern California with an outdoor long-course pool. Needless to say, the plans and schedules laid for these two situations would differ. All too often schedules are copied with no consideration for geographical conditions.

Time

Our place in time, the date, and the availability of time, are generally outside our control. This is year X and the County record is Y secs. That time is the time to beat in the swimmer's mind. True, planning must look to the future, but goals must be based on current reality. Goals and goal setting are a natural product of the consideration of time and are considered later in the planning of training and competition. Time availability, i.e., swimmers' time, teacher/coach time, water time, are all limiting factors in some way, but it is amazing how determination can change factors thought to be beyond control. Facilities can be a major planning problem. A particular pool length is a necessity for competition swimming at certain levels. Again, determination can play its part in surmounting the seemingly insurmountable.

Gender

This is a major factor, particularly in certain countries and under certain religious regimes. Equality and emancipation are playing their part slowly and surely, but there is little sign so far that, except in rare cases, biological factors have been overcome. Male muscle still has greater strength than female muscle.

Annual Planning

The picture is more easily understood when applied specifically to swimming, or perhaps a swimmer, as an annual plan. It all begins with, "Here I am with an ambition".

Performance requirements

These are competitions outside the control of the swimmer and swum to certain known, and unchangeable, rules. It is known, for example, that the Olympic Games is held every four years and the conditions binding the races are known. That must be a major planning consideration.

Individual potential

The swimmer is there "as seen"; there is no point, in planning, to wish s/he were ten inches taller. Plans are made for a given, particular individual.

Stage of training

This is something which cannot be altered. Again, the teacher/coach cannot go back in time; a swimmer with one year's training must follow a training plan appropriate to that age, aptitude and ability.

The Training Plan

The training plan is a complete programme of "cycles of training", punctuated by tests and competitions. The questions the coach must answer are:
- What to apply to stimulate training?
- When to apply the stimulus?
- How much to apply?
- How to apply it?

The "What?" and "How?" are outlined in "Methods of training". The "When?" and "How much?" are matters for planning.

Figure 8.2 The Training Plan – Annual

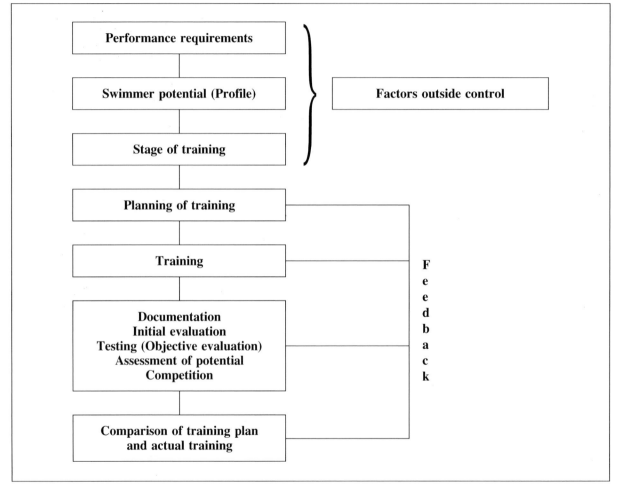

Training Cycles

A training programme consists of:

- ● an aim;
- ● a preparation phase;
- ● a phase of training exercises related to the aim;

- a phase of competition or performance;
- a phase of rest, recovery, regeneration and review; (4Rs)

This is a cyclic pattern (see Fig. 8.3) which is followed no matter what the length of the training period, from a number of years down to one session. The phases are of equal importance and, particularly the latter, namely, the 4R's phase of rest, recovery, regeneration and review.

By observing the basic training principles of adaptation and progressive overload, each cycle must reflect the developing and improving condition of the swimmer, i.e., each aim must have higher goals than its predecessor.

Figure 8.3 A three cycle year for a national class swimmer peaking for winter championships, GB Club championships and summer championships

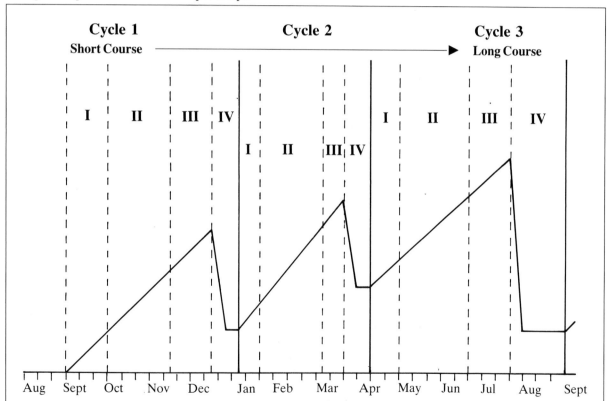

I	Preparation period
II	Training exercise period
III	Competition period
IV	Rest, recovery, regeneration and review

A long term cycle is generally four years, and is controlled by a major event such as the Olympic Games. Although there are only a few swimmers directly concerned, this particular cycle spreads downwards through the positioning of events at national and district levels, and so down to County and Club competitions. Whether or not this should be so is a philosophical question, and answered by the one word **"motivation"**. These major events provide the inspiration and the spur, and it is only right that they should hold an exalted position of control in the master plan. Elite, senior swimmers tend to plan their careers in these long term cycles. For most younger swimmers the cycles are usually one year long, although there are, occasionally, those wise old heads on young shoulders who can pitch their vision many years forward and keep it clearly in view. Often these are the true champions. No matter what the length of the cycle, a review is an essential and it is wise to do it after a period of rest, preferably following success, or at least following a satisfying season. Decisions should never be made when physical condition and feelings are at a low ebb.

Annual planning, if the basics have been observed, is one of the most exciting times in a teacher/coach year. No two years are identical, and it follows that no two annual plans are the same. Conversely, it is true that, in any one geographical area, there are many items in annual planning which are the same year in year out. The dominating external influences tend to change very little. Finding changes which can produce a more exciting plan is all part of the teacher/coach work.

It is useful and convenient for teachers/coaches to set out a pattern for the annual plan. Fig. 8.4 on page 89 is an example of such a plan. Dates can be inserted, and the plan followed day by day so that, at any moment, the teacher/coach can see the precise point he is at in the programme. For those with a particular interest in planning, it is not difficult to construct an even more elaborate device with moving arrows. Coupled with an annual wall planner, it is an excellent method of keeping on course.

It is the task of the teacher/coach to search out all events of influence in an approaching year and then, in consultation with the swimmer, carefully start planning by first inserting the major events, followed by the supporting competitions. Strategies, the "When?" and "How much?", are then developed according to both the swimmer's capabilities and those of the support systems. The "What?" and "How?" are, at this stage, in outline only. It is neither possible nor desirable to plan method and material in any detail.

After that stage the plan should be presented to the appropriate body, e.g., the Club committee, responsible for organisation, administration and, of course, finance. Support can be planned and, if necessary, modifications made. The task of this body is to study feasibility of the plans and to decide how best to provide maximum back up. Grandiose plans are fine, but if they cannot be supported they are doomed. The involvement at this stage of all parties concerned is essential to a trouble-free operation. Similarly, as the year unfolds, changes are certain to be necessary and it is vital that all concerned are informed and involved. This means, therefore, the setting up of formal channels of communication. Clubs should ensure that all appropriate personnel, and this must include the teacher/coach, are on the committee.

The placing of the "When?" and the "How?" is best achieved by planning backwards from the major events, in both time and the expected level of condition of the swimmer, e.g., "By this date swimmer X should be doing this type of training and achieving this type of performance." The process continues backwards until the beginning of the cycle is reached and that cycle is complete.

Aim

The training cycle must have an aim which must be in accordance with the age, aptitude and ability of the swimmer and must be administratively achieveable.

Figure 8.4 Planning from long to short term including a three cycle year

Long term ambition in years							
Aim 1	2	3	4	5	6	7	8

Annual plan		
Cycle (Term) I Aim	Cycle (Term) II Aim	Cycle (Term) III Aim

Cycle I														
Preparation			Main conditioning						Competition			4 "Rs"		
1	2	3*	4	5*	6	7	8*	9	10*	11*	12*	13	14	15

*Testing and/or competition

Cycle I showing 15 weeks in five sub-groups of three weeks for each of preparation, aerobic emphasis, intensive emphasis, competition specific, rest, recovery, regeneration and review (4Rs)

Week 6						
1 M	2 T	3 W	4 Th	5 F	6 Sa	` 7 Su

Day 3	
am	pm

Preparation phase

The preparation phase is the first part of the cycle. It is here that the swimmer makes the necessary adjustments to body and mind and, possibly, lifestyle, to cope with the demands of future training. The length of the phase depends upon two factors:

● the degree of inactivity of the preceding 4R's phase or other breaks caused possibly by illness, injury or other commitments;
● the length and intensity of the next phase.

The preparation phase at the beginning of a year tends to be the longest. The greatest emphasis is on technique, at first with conditioning as an outcome of technique training, but later with conditioning becoming more important with the development of aerobic capacity as the main concern. There should be a testing period at the end of the preparation phase.

Main training phase

The move out of the preparation period must be a smooth transition into the main training phase. Sudden changes in the type and intensity of training can cause a state of failing adaptation.

Methods of training in this phase will reflect more specifically the demands of the future performance requirements which are generally in four categories of specialisation, i.e., Children or age group; Distance 1500m 800m; Middle distance 400m IM 400m 200m; Sprint 100m 50m.

Children up to the age of 12/13 years of age should be concentrating on a broad range of activity to develop **technique, basic speed** and **aerobic capacity** (see Fig. 8.5).

Figure 8.5 Main content and balance of "training" for children aged 8-12 ±1 year

Areas for development	No. of sessions per week	Activities	Competition	Mental development aims
Technique All strokes; starts; turns; finishes and takeovers. Skills associated with all disciplines and, in particular, sculling and use of legs	2-3 ↓	See "Methods of Training"	3-4 Per year ↓	1. Basic understanding 2. Love of the sport and of exercise in general 3. Learn to appreciate the benefits of swimming 4. Developing the habits of a healthy lifestyle 5. Sportsmanship and a sense of fair play 6. Learning harmonious association with others
Basic speed Reaction time; stroke length and "feel"; swimming fast for short distances and swimming is fun				
Aerobic Capacity Sub-maximal short distances/short rest; building to distance with sound technique	4-5		12 Per year	

90

The balance of training for the older age group and senior swimmers is outlined in Fig. 8.6. It must be stressed that the percentages given in the chart are guidelines only.

Figure 8.6 Balance of training – guidelines

Percentage of Energy System Training						
Purpose → ↓ (Specialist event)	Relaxation	Recovery	Maintenance	Anaerobic Threshold and stress	Speed Endurance (anaerobic lactic acid)	Sprint (ATP/CP)
50m	25%	10%	20%	20%	5%	20%
↓	10%	20%	30%	30%	5-10% ⇄	10-5%
	10%	20%	25%	30%	10%	5%
	10%	15%	25%	35%	10%	5%
800m/1500m	10%	10%	35%	35%	5%	5%

The emphasis on the first half of the phase will be on developing aerobic capacity, moving towards speed endurance in the second phase. Figure 8.6 tends to strike an average.

Competition phase
Minor competitions punctuate all phases of training but they become more dominant in the next phase of the cycle. The number, spacing, intensity, prominence and variety of competitions must be considered carefully. Some events will be chosen to test certain aspects of performance, such as pacing, others for qualifying times. Yet, again, others will be selected for various psychological reasons. No matter what the purpose of the competition, it must be stressed that the **aim of any race is to win.** Sometimes, in practising or experimenting, race placing may not be as high as expected, but this is all part of the build up. However, any experiment loses its value unless the effort is made to win and swimmers must always be reminded that this effort is essential; equally, they must not be depressed by losing.

There are occasions when a swimmer is selected to represent club, school or even country. It is the duty of both the teacher/coach and the swimmer to contact, without delay, the selection body in order to inform and clarify the state of training and expectations. Equally, the various organisations must make their position clear, at the same time respecting the wishes and rights of the swimmer. Intentions and plans of both parties must be made clear so that recriminations are avoided.

Another problem associated with this phase is an over emphasis on competition and speed endurance training, causing a deterioration in basic aerobic fitness and consequent detraining. This is essentially a phase of careful surveillance and judicious testing.

Rest, recovery, regeneration and review (4Rs)
The fourth phase is one of rest, recovery, regeneration and review, and is one so often ignored and neglected. The history of teaching/coaching has been dogged by the "hard work – all sacrifice" philosophy,

and teachers/coaches, by tradition, are inclined toward this belief. The result is often constant pressure and no relaxation.

In every annual plan there should be clear breaks long enough to permit the necessary 4Rs. Over many years the body clock, the swimmer's regular mental and physical habits, becomes accustomed to a pattern of living. In some parts of the world it may be primitive and governed by nature. In modern circumstances however, the annual pattern has grown up around certain festivals and accepted breaks. It is natural, therefore, that the swimming calendar, and the cycles of training, fit this annual pattern by making this all important resting phase coincide with the traditional breaks wherever possible. The rest period can take many forms, from total passive rest and relaxation to activity rests which are simply a complete change. Following this rest, recovery and regeneration is the review, the final act of one cycle and at the same time the basis of the next.

The three cycle year seems to be the most advantageous. The human body, provided it is free of illness, well-nourished, content and has sufficient rest, responds to training stimuli comparatively rapidly. The first two to three weeks of training produces the most rapid development and, gradually, this rate of progress steadily levels off. Changes in training and fresh stimuli must be introduced to produce further surges of development. Planning must use this, the body's natural development cycle, to determine the length of the various training cycles. Broad calculations show that building in time periods of three weeks, three or four complete training cycles a year are possible.

Bearing in mind the various influences, e.g., commitments such as examinations, the three cycle year seems the most appropriate. Some swimmers have a total commitment to swimming. They are unfettered by career, work, academic or family influences. The cycles in these cases may be different but, for the majority of swimmers, the three cycle year is still the most beneficial. Each of the cycles of 12 to 15 weeks then breaks down naturally into those smaller periods of three weeks or so in which the greatest development takes place.

Clearly, the above is only a sketchy outline. So much depends upon those factors beyond control, e.g., swimmer profile, water-time facilities and the various commitments suggested earlier; all play a part in designing a realistic plan. In general, those with less time in the water require longer cycles to show improvement. It is the task of the teacher/coach and swimmer to consider the training emphasis.

The weekly cycle

The weekly cycle is a further breakdown of the cycles of planning into periods of training and emphasizes the fulfilling of the requirements of the general aim. The weekly cycle is most obviously and directly affected by school and job demands and the availability of pool-time. The most important aspects of weekly planning are variety and the balance of intensities of training with rest periods. The plan must ensure that the swimmer is always ready to get the most from every training session by avoiding boredom and overtraining. Like all other cycles the weekly plan must have aims. Fig. 8.7 shows two examples. The main aim of the former, (a), is the development of endurances particularly applicable to a period of building basic aerobic endurance. The latter, (b), exemplifies a week of a later period when speed endurance becomes a main feature. The height of the columns indicate the degree of intensity for that session.

The degree of intensity applies not only to the energy systems as outlined in Fig. 8.7(a) and (b) on page 93. Every facet of training, technique, speed, power and flexibility, must have similar emphases to ensure those essentials of variety, work and recovery.

It is not necessary, at this stage, to plan each session in detail. Planning of detailed schedules weeks in

Figure 8.7(a) and (b) – Examples of weekly plans

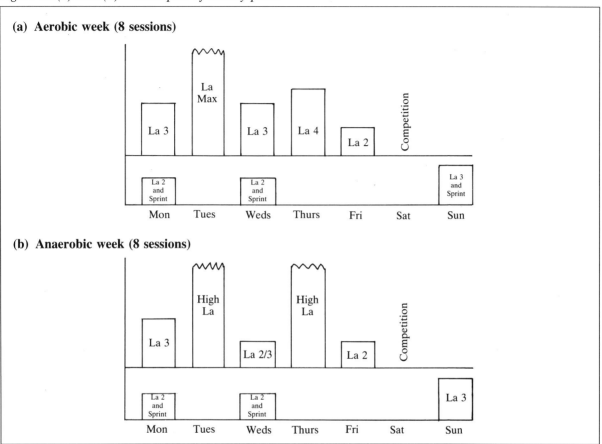

KEY: La = Intensity in terms of lactate level

advance, or even a week in advance, should be avoided. It is important to be clear how the week fits the general plans and how the emphasis each day fits the plan for the week.

The training session/schedule

The smallest unit in the plan is what has become known as the **training session** or **schedule.** This is a training exercise, or a series of exercises, which are a recognisable part of an overall plan leading to an ultimate goal. There are certain essential features:

● above all, the schedule must be planned in advance, with less and less detail the further away the planning takes place. This allows maximum adherence to the overall plan with maximum flexibility or ability to adjust;

93

- an **aim** which is known to both teacher/coach and swimmer. All activities must support that aim;
- the schedule must be satisfying, enjoyable and appropriate to the needs of the individual in the particular conditions;
- there must be **understanding** and **motivation.** Both teacher/coach and swimmer must know the purpose of each activity and be motivated to achieving the best outcome. A sense of purpose must be apparent;
- it must show **progression;**
- the exercises must be **compatible.** The teacher/coach must know which types of training do not mix well;
- there must be an appropriate **balance** and **placing** of intensity and recovery;
- there must be **harmonious variety.** Variety must not disrupt flow or create fragmentation and, consequently, lose sight of the aim;
- the session must fit the time available or satisfaction and effect is lost;
- each activity must be given enough time for maximum effect. In short sessions of one hour or less it is important to plan and, where necessary, carefully limit the aims.
- **monitoring is essential;**
- copying and using schedules from other sources should be avoided, however, **use good ideas and always acknowledge them.**

Recording the schedule

Writing down the schedule in a legible, logical manner is part of the professionalism of teaching/coaching and a "page-a-day" diary is excellent for this purpose, Each teacher/coach will wish to use his or her own system for writing a schedule, but the following is a suggestion:

- **Aim** clearly written at the top of the page
  – Set the page out as follows:

  Example

No. of reps		length of rep.	Stroke		Rest	Instructions
6	×	400	F/C	with	30	at (pace)

- **Further notes** written immediately after the schedule;
- **Personal assessment** space left after the written plan for further notes on the session.

Monitoring

Monitoring during all phases of planning is vital. There is an **initial subjective assessment,** a "feeling" for the effect. This is often at its greatest after a daily training session.

Testing and objective evaluation

Testing and objective evaluation is a more accurate method of deciding whether or not the result was as planned or as believed to be. Adopting these procedures means that records must be kept in order to provide an element of control.

Comparison of plan and outcome

Finally, in the annual cycle, there must be a comparison of the training plan and what actually happened, such is the nature of change and readjustment, "If the original plan and what actually happened are the same, then something is wrong". (Rushton C., (1991) "High Yield Workouts", Vancouver Conference).

Goal setting

Goal setting is an obvious part of planning. Unfortunately it is so obvious that it is often taken for granted and expressed in the vaguest of terms. It requires training, i.e., simple instructions to ensure that goals are attainable and not just a path to disappointment. Young swimmers should be encouraged as soon as possible to set themselves targets and to put them in **writing.**

Writing down targets is the most important factor in goal setting. In the early learning stages of swimming setting targets is not difficult. Good, progressive award schemes are available. They begin with the first few strokes, progress through the various skills and on to short distance speed awards. In searching for suitable schemes teachers/coaches should observe certain essentials:

- motivation for the scheme – select the award schemes with extreme care;
- beware of a multiplicity of awards – they become meaningless and even bewildering;
- schemes must be truly progressive;
- minor awards should be frequently attainable;
- award must follow achievement as quickly as is possible;
- cost to the swimmer should be carefully considered.

Eventually a stage or age is reached when badges are no longer an incentive and young swimmers need to find their own goals. Swimmers can be assisted by:

- studying local, well-known standards;
- using results of slightly higher grade competition as a yardstick;
- keeping an accurate record of personal best times;
- using team selection as a goal;
- using competition qualifying times as a target;
- aiming to break records;
- aiming for championship titles.

It will be noted that beating certain opponents is not listed because it is an aim for each and every race – **the objective of a race is to win.** The "elimination" of opponents, however, is fraught with danger. In this situation the target is "moving" and also striving for greater achievement. Hitting a "moving" target is always more difficult, particularly if it knows that it is a target and takes appropriate measures not to be hit!

Teachers/coaches must be wary of the "intermediate goal" problem in which the swimmer, in achieving a tough intermediate goal, loses sight of the main objective. It is most often seen at national level when the intermediate goal of, say, selection for the Olympic Team, satisfies either, or both, swimmer and teacher/coach who think that they have "arrived" and, consequently, lose sight of the higher goals.

Using a combination of measures is probably the best way forward, but underlying it all is the basic principle, "Set targets high, but reach them in small steps." Many small bites make a large meal. High goals, in themselves, are capable of frightening the swimmer, but broken down into small steps of improvement they can become achievable.

Finally, goal setting has wider applications than simply achieving times. This wider application should not be forgotten, e.g., attendance or dietary goals.

Chapter 9

Age Group Swimming

Steve Greenfield

Introduction

Technically, age group swimming means that swimmers are grouped together according to their age, (usually based on December 31st in the year of competition) to compete in specific swimming events. Age group training schemes consist of groups of swimmers grouped together by age and ability for the purpose of training to compete in swimming events. Swimmers will usually enter a competitive programme after a period of teaching/coaching, ranging from 6 months to 2 years. Most programmes accept swimmers from the age of 7 or 9 years. For the purpose of this chapter, the age range of swimmers will be from 7 to 14 years. The competitive aims of swimmers within this age bracket will range from stroke improvement to Age Group National competition.

The motivation for attending the teaching/coaching sessions will vary considerably: from those who enjoy the social function of a club, and wish to swim in a recreational fashion, to those who wish to attain competitive success. The teacher/coach will need to assess the developmental age and training needs of each swimmer. Whilst s/he must be aware of the most up-to-date methods of teaching/coaching and training, a subjective judgement still needs to be made as to the needs of individual swimmers. There is little point in using advanced techniques with swimmers who only swim once a week for 45 minutes and whose competitive aim is to be able to swim 25 metres on each stroke.

Swimming, following the principles of all training, requires periods of increased workloads during which the swimmer adapts to these increases. To this must be added periods of continuous stroke assessment and grooming. Age group swimming differs from working with more senior swimmers in that, in the former, the athlete is constantly changing and growing physically and mentally at all times. This makes the job of the teacher/coach of age group swimmers extremely challenging. A swimmer who is entering a period of increased growth will often exhibit signs of failing adaptation to training and their ability to swim the strokes correctly will decrease. It is during these phases, particularly around the age of puberty, that swimmers feel that somehow they are not trying hard enough and embark on suicidal amounts of hard training, often compounding the problems. There is some evidence from Eastern European Countries which suggests that increased rest and reduced training levels is the best reaction to these phases of growth. Common sense and constant observation, i.e. knowing the swimmers, will reveal when there is a problem. The teacher/ coach reaction should be calculated on what is best for the swimmer and not necessarily the team. Some swimmers will mature in spurts, while others will grow at a constant rate. Age group teachers/coaches, therefore, need to understand both the mental and physical development of their swimmers.

Age related workload

The topic of "How much? How young?" has caused many arguments between teachers/coaches and physicians over the years and there still remains no definite formula for success. One example of a workload

Figure 9.1 A guide for age group coaching

Training age		Year 1	Year 2	Year 3	Year 4	Year 5+
Actual age		8–10 years	10–12 years	12–14 years	13–15 years	14+ years
Swim sessions/week		2–3	3–4	4–6	5–7	6–8
Duration of session		45 mins-1 hour	1 hour	1-1½ hours	1½-2 hours	1½-2 hours
Distance per hour		400-1200m	1000-2000m	1500-2600m	2000-3500m	2000-5000m
Types of training swimming		Skills and drills Basic speed work Reactions Aerobic	Interval training aerobic endurance Advanced drills Alactic work	TIS Aerobic/threshold Strength endurance	All energy systems Power training Lactate testing (Girls)	As year 4, but increased to suit individuals (Including boys)
Make up of training	Technical	85%	45%	25%	15%	Dependent on individual requirements
	Aerobic		35%	55%	65%	
	Sprint	15%	20%	15%	15%	
	Anaerobic	0%	0%	5%	5%	
Other activities		1 × 30 mins session/week Aerobic work Co-ordination skills	2 × 30 mins session/week Aerobic work including flexibility and running	3 × 30 mins session/week As Year 2 plus muscular endurance	2 hours/week As Year 3 plus low intensity weights dependent on physical maturation	Dependent on individual requirements
Education		The starting procedure Reading the pace clock Basic stroke laws Poolside safety Health and hygiene Lane discipline	Read and record times. Basic principles of training. The TIS swim. Stroke counting. The ASA laws and racing Goal setting	Methods and principles of training for the coming season Race strategy Basic nutrition	Fully conversant with all swim related topics including sports injury. Basic relaxation technique Mental rehearsal	New topics Teaching skills Life skills Personal development
Competition		Short sprints 12.5-25m on a time trial basis within club	Internal and local club competition	Club and district level up to county	County up to national dependent on ability	National to international dependent on ability
Categorisation		By ability in groups	By ability in groups and lanes	Early preferences and abilities noted	Early specialisation by ability tailored to suit individual needs	Specialisation dependent on ability
Season length		Year round with holiday breaks	Based on school terms with clear breaks	10 months with defined seasons	10 months with seasons based around major competition	8-10 months based individual requirements and school examinations

Key: TIS = Training interval swim

is suggested at Fig. 9.1 on page 97. Whilst this table gives a general rule it is by no means intended to be strictly followed. Clearly, some swimmers will reach physical maturity well before others and, by the same token, many will lag behind and be labelled late developers. It is for this reason that the table gives an actual age range for each developmental stage as well as a training age. Training age is the number of years a swimmer has been involved in competition training, e.g., 2 swimmers begin training at a club, one 8 and one 10 years of age. After 2 years of preliminary training both will have a training age of 2 years. The choice of which system to adopt is up to the individual teacher/coach. Common sense, however, dictates that a 15 year old who has only been swimming for 1 year will not be treated in the same way as an 8 year old after 1 year. Fig. 9.1 also details suggested methods of testing to be undertaken to assess training speed and cruise intervals. Testing should be started as soon as possible for it is on sound, physical testing methods that success will be built.

Fig. 9.1 gives training ages from 1 to 5+ years with actual age range of between 8 and 14 years. If the column headed training, age 3, can be taken as an example, the following interpretation could be given:

- amounts of training and times in the pool are dependent, not only age but also the position within the training cycle. For example, swimmers approaching a major competition would not be covering the maximum distances given in the table;
- types of training will vary according to the facilities and time available. It must be stressed that, even with limited time, all elements of training should be covered to give a balanced programme;
- other activities can be structured around the facilities available. If a gymnasium is not available a corridor in winter, or an outside area in summer, can provide an excellent alternative;
- education material should be linked to the topics being used by the swimmers in the pool, e.g., principles of basic conditioning. Educational material used should be suitable for children and basic in its content. Schools and Colleges might be useful sources of information;
- competition should be fun with realistic aims for performance. The levels given are a maximum, not what should have been achieved;
- categorisation is where swimmers are grouped according to stroke or distance preference. Training, however, should include work on all strokes and distances.

Fig. 9.2 on page 99 is a suggested plan of training based around a six week cycle, showing an overall theme of work for early season training. This guide has been used for a group of swimmers with a training age of between 2 and 3 years, having reached a physical maturity of between 10 and 12 years of age. A whole year can be built around 4, 6 and 8 week cycles allowing for major events and school holidays. It requires much more planning and recording but the results are worth the extra work.

Types of training

Success with age group swimmers is gained by not only stimulating the body but also the mind. Even the most structured programme with swimmers working physically very hard is wasted if it allows no mental involvement. The development of physical prowess goes hand in hand with increased understanding and knowledge.

Part II of this book will make teachers/coaches aware of the principles of work and rest, adaptation to work and the various types of work undertaken by swimmers; for example, overdistance, interval, lactate production and ATP sprint work. To perform these types of sets correctly the swimmers need to acquire a certain amount of knowledge about themselves and their pool environment. This can be encouraged from

Figure 9.2 Six week training plan – Front Crawl development (early season)

Training type	Week 1	Week 2	Week 3	Week 4	Week 5	Week 6
Warm up	800m Mix swim to include drills	600m Front Crawl swim	400m Front Crawl catch up or mixed drills	400m Own choice swim	600m Mixed drills	400m Front Crawl to Back Crawl
Main sets	100m + swims sets of 600m max RI 30 secs 60-70% effort	150m swims F/C sets of 600m max RI 30 secs 65-75% effort	Fartlek work 4 × 400m F/C every 3rd 25m sprint 12.5m RI 30 secs	200s F/C or IM 1000m sets RI 20-30 secs	F/C sets of 100 10 × 100m TTPB 20→15secs on 2.00 mins	F/C sets of 100 10 × 100m TTPB 15→10secs on 3.00 mins
Sectional contrast work	Medley end swims 100m last 12.5m IM + drill swims	Kick sets 100m swims O/C 4 × 100 RI 30 + drill swims	Kick sets 200m swims F/C sets of 3-4 RI 30-60 secs	Kick sets 200m swims F/C or O/C sets of 800m RI 30 secs	medley work 100m→25m strokes drill work kick 50 hard 30-45 RI	Mixed IM 100m drills 50m O/C pull 50m RI 30 secs
Sprint work		2×alactic (ATP) sets 10 × 12.5m max sprints 25m on 1 min	2×alactic (ATP) sets 10 × 12.5m max sprints 25m on 1 min			1×alactic (ATP) sets 10 × 12.5m max sprints 25m on 1 min
Notes	Emphasize technique hand and head position No swims under 50m. No relays	Drills to be specific with an aim Fill session with mixed IM work	More drills Build distance	Challenge set Max distance day How many 200m swims can you do? RI 15 secs	Slightly reduce distance More fun relays	Technique Hand and head position 200m time trial at weekend

Key: F/C = Front Crawl; O/C = Own choice; IM = Individual Medley; RI = Repeat interval; TTPB = Target time personal best.

a very early age and once learned is never forgotten. Below are examples of how to increase knowledge and create good habits.

First training year – example

In addition to developing sound swimming skills, swimmers should be introduced to:

- correct race procedures, e.g., every time they are asked to enter the water the swimmers should stand back from the side, move to the edge on the command, "Take your marks!" and react to a starting signal. Similarly, there should be insistence on the correct turning and finishing procedures, e.g., driving into the wall and powerful stretched and streamlined pushes away from the wall;

- reading the pace clock, e.g., encourage the swimmers to look at the clock on starting and finishing a task. The important thing is that they look and are aware of the point of starting and finishing. Make sure the pace clock has clearly defined symbols, if possible numbered or with coloured segments;

- knowledge of the appropriate swimming laws.

Second training year – example

Swimmers should be able to record accurately their own time from the pace clock. They should also be able to swim a set of repeats on a given swim/rest time. Games and relay races can be devised around the use of the pace clock.

Example: (swimmers in teams)
– first swimmer swims 25m from a whistle or gun and then gets out of the pool and tells the next swimmer the time s/he has taken to cover the 25m, e.g., 21 seconds;
– next swimmer dives in at 21 seconds from the 60 on the clock and then gets out and tells the next swimmer the time taken, (e.g., 19 seconds);
– the next swimmers leaves at 19 seconds from the 60 on the clock and so on. After each length swimmers write their own times on a board. The winning team has the lowest total time. Teams are penalised 5 seconds for leaving on the wrong time or misreading the clock. There are many variations on this theme and the coach should be inventive, not forgetting that the aim is to teach swimmers how to use the pace clock.

Swimmers should be introduced to:

● the principles of basic conditioning, e.g., Why they need to train to improve physical performance. An introduction to some relevant terminology to be used during the coming years, including interval training, aerobics and anaerobic conditioning, etc, should be undertaken at this stage;

● stroke counting. All swimmers should be aware of the number of strokes they require to complete each length of the pool on each of the strokes they swim. An explanation of the mechanics of the stroke can be undertaken with reference to the stroke and distance principle. When using stroke counting as a training method care should be taken to avoid swimmers using a kick dominated stroke to achieve a reduced stroke count for each length. The aim and reasons for using stroke counting should be explained before the start of the set.

Third training year – example

● swimmers should be aware of all the methods and principles of training that they will be using during the season's work. The swimmers can be allowed input into the training schedules by deciding on what sets they want to swim providing they can give the reasoning behind their choice. Whether cruise intervals based on Personal Best time (PB) plus a percentage effort, based on a T30 swim, or blood lactate analysis is being used, swimmers should know their own times.

Fourth training year – example

● each swimmer should be conversant with swimming and training principles, including preparation and relaxation techniques. From this point, education will be based on the specific requirements of the swimmers with the aim of developing self-reliance.

The use of specific drills

Drills are often used to perfect a particular aspect of swimming technique from the simplest kicking drill to complex breathing drills. They are often used to give swimmers a break from routine but, unfortunately, they often lack purpose and progression. Swimmers need to have a stated aim, e.g., swim a head-up Front Crawl drill to see hand entry position and work on the catch phase of the stroke. The same head-up drill, often called "Water Polo" stroke, can also be used to develop speed of arm turnover if the specific aim is stated. Progression is a very important part of drill swimming. A drill that is challenging to start with will often become easy and usually non-productive after a while. The following shows a progression in Back Crawl kicking drills:

- Kick on back, hands at side;
- Kick on back, hands extended above head. Streamline position;
- Kick on side, one arm extended above head and other arm at side;
- Kick 6 on side, 6 on back and 6 on other side;
- Kick on back, arms out of water at 45 degree angle to body;
- Kick on back, arms out of water at 90 degrees angle to body;
- Kick on back with weight belt, hands across chest;
- Kick on back with weight belt, arms extended above head.

The above drills are all progressive and, depending on the type of use and distance covered, they can have totally different effects. The first drill shown, for example, could be used with a swimmer who has not yet mastered the mechanics required to perform the second drill on the list. It could also be used with very proficient Back Crawl swimmers as a relaxation. Alternatively, it could be used with good swimmers swimming sets of 100m repeats where the body position and kick mechanics would break down if the streamlined position of the second drill was adopted.

Swimmers enjoy difficult tasks. If a drill is too easy they will soon lose interest and, likewise, if a drill is unattainable they will also lose interest. Most drills are multi-purpose, and the swimmers must be aware of the precise purpose of each drill as it is set.

Example: The Front Crawl catch up drill has many uses. Some are listed below:

1. To promote body position streamlining;
2. To promote length of stroke;
3. To promote high elbow recovery by isolation;
4. To work on the initial catch on the water;
5. As a kicking drill;
6. To work on head position.

There are, therefore, at least 6 tasks or 6 separate drills.

The drills used will be designed and tailor-made by the teacher/coach to suit the needs of his/her swimmers. Providing there are no inherent unsafe or hazardous practices, the teacher/coach should not be afraid to experiment with drills in order to achieve an aim or bring something fresh to a session.

Equipment

So far simple drills using no aids have been suggested. Some currently available swim aids that teachers/coaches may find useful are shown in Fig. 9.3. All of the above have uses for which they were designed but, as with drills, their use can be made specific to the needs of individual swimmers. The object of all drill swimming, and the use of swim aids, is to produce swimmers who can swim the competitive strokes **fast in competition.**

Figure 9.3 Swimming aids and possible uses

Kick boards (various sizes)	These can be used for leg work as well as isolating single arm drills
Pullbuoy	These can be used for pulling work as well as assisting body position
Fins (flippers)	Fins can be used to promote leg mechanics and strength, to increase ankle flexibility or to give extra speed for assisted swimming (cut down fins are particularly useful for assisted speed swimming)
Hand paddles Arm paddles Finger paddles	Paddles can be used for any swimming drill but are normally used for strength and stroke mechanics improvement, e.g., arm paddles can help promote high elbow position in the Front Crawl stroke
Ankle tube	These are used to isolate the legs in a pulling drill. They can be used with or without a pullbuoy
Wrist and ankle weights Weight belts	Weight belts and wrist and ankle belts are used for strength building only. They are not recommended for use with young swimmers or for those who do not have excellent stroke mechanics
Stretch cords	The cords are used for resistance training (Tethered swimming). Coupled with stroke counting they are very useful for simulating long course (50m) swims in a short course (25m) pool

Chapter 10

Safety

John Lawton

Introduction

For those swimmers who have developed sound basic strokes it is often necessary to move from a class organisation, based upon width swimming, to one which necessitates the swimmers completing lengths. This is a natural progression and should be encouraged, particularly for those swimmers who may wish to participate competitively.

Swimming in lanes

Dividing the pool through the use of lane ropes enables the maximum use to be made of the water space available, and also enables the swimmers to swim lengths in comparative safety. Once the pool is divided into lanes the swimmers generally follow a "chain", or "circuit pattern", with each lane usually swimming in opposite directions, as in Fig. 10.1.

Figure 10.1 Lane swimming

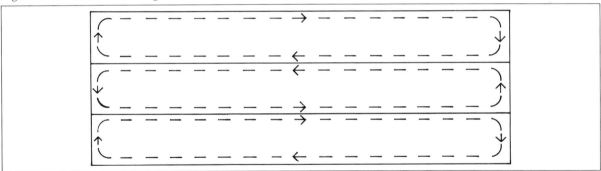

However, there are occasions, provided that the lane is wide enough, when the swimmers in each lane may swim side by side. This is commonly referred to as "wave" swimming, but this method can only be utilised when performing one length swims or when the other swimmers in the lane wait on the poolside until the swim is completed. "Wave" swimming is not always the most efficient use of space, but is particularly useful if the swimmers are concentrating upon speed work.

Lane discipline

Irrespective of the type of lane organisation adopted by the teacher/coach it is vitally important to ensure that swimmers are taught the principles and practice of lane discipline. This will contribute towards the safety of the swimmers and, hopefully, avoid unnecessary accidents. Arguably, the most important factor relating to the safe conduct of lane swimming is the number of swimmers in each lane. It is impossible to give a definitive statement on this as there are so many variables, including the size of pool, the size and age of swimmer, the ability of swimmer, and the nature of the swimming being undertaken etc. However, in order that the swimmers achieve the maximum benefit from the session being conducted, and are able to swim in a safe manner, it should be possible to complete the set distances without undue interference from fellow swimmers. If a swimmer's "flow" is constantly being interrupted through contact with others there is a good chance that there are too many swimmers in a lane, and both the effectiveness of the session and safety of the swimmer will be impaired.

Number of swimmers in a lane

In a training situation a rough guide to the number of swimmers in a lane can be arrived at by utilising the following equation. This assumes that the swimmers are roughly of the same ability.

Example: Repetitions on 50 metres

$$\frac{\text{Time of Repetition}}{\text{Interval between starts}} = \text{Number of swimmers in a lane}$$

- $\dfrac{60 \text{ secs}}{5 \text{ secs}} = 12 \text{ swimmers}$ - $\dfrac{60 \text{ secs}}{10 \text{ secs}} = 6 \text{ swimmers}$

Example: Repetitions above 50 metres (working in a 25 metres pool)

Obviously, the last swimmer in a lane must have started before the first swimmer has completed the first 50 metres. Therefore, for repetitions of 100 metres the equation would be:

$$\frac{\text{Average time for 2 lengths (50 metres)}}{\text{Interval between starts}} = \text{Number of swimmers in a lane}$$

- $\dfrac{35 \text{ secs}}{5 \text{ secs}} = 7 \text{ swimmers}$ - $\dfrac{50 \text{ secs}}{10 \text{ secs}} = 5 \text{ swimmers}$

Key points for lane swimming

- all swimmers need to be clear about the direction of travel;
- teachers/coaches should ensure that the ability of the swimmers in each lane is similar. It is important to note that this may necessitate some changes depending on the activity;
- have a clear and well understood policy for dealing with the situation in which one swimmer catches up with another. Possible solutions to this are:
  - the swimmer being caught completes a length and then waits until overtaken. This can result in the slower swimmers experiencing constant interruptions and, therefore, possibly losing some of the beneficial effects of the particular session;
  - the overtaking swimmer crosses over into a space before reaching the end of the pool. Distance or time benefits can be lost in this situation;
  - sufficient space is left in the middle of the lane to allow for overtaking. This increases the possibility of swimmer colliding and is potentially dangerous.

NB. No matter which system is adopted it needs to be clearly understood and followed by **all** the swimmers.

- teachers/coaches need to give careful consideration to the particular strokes which swimmers are asked to perform when swimming in lanes, and to decide when it is advantageous or detrimental to mix strokes. In many pools, for example, where the lanes are quite narrow, the strokes with wide arm actions can cause accidents. It may be, therefore, that on those occasions where the pool is particularly busy, some mixing of strokes might be helpful. Adopting a system whereby swimmers complete one length Butterfly, followed by one on Back Crawl, repeatedly, will help to overcome this particular problem. The important point is that time has been given to thinking through a variety of organisational structures which will enable the swimmer to complete the set tasks without the risk of injury;

- the increased use of goggles for swimming training can help towards the individual's awareness of other swimmers in the lane. Swimmers should be constantly encouraged to use the improved underwater visibility provided by goggles to help towards a safer environment. However, goggles can lead to eye injury if inexperienced swimmers are not given clear instructions as to how to put them on and take them off in a safe manner. It is important to **explain the potential dangers** of lifting the goggles away from the eyes in order to demist the lenses. It is quite possible for an inexperienced user of goggles, particularly if the hands are cold, to allow the goggles to "catapult" into the eye and cause serious damage;

- swimming Back Crawl presents more difficulties than the other three strokes since there is an increased possibility of collision with other swimmers and with the ends of the pool. Keeping to the side of each lane will prevent any collision and, in order to avoid unnecessary injury caused through collision with the ends of the pool, swimmers should be taught:
  - to look for marks above the swimming pool and use these for guidance;
  - to be aware of the purpose of the 5m turning flags and count strokes to the wall. It is not surprising that many swimmers who have not been specifically taught about turning flags do actually think that they are for decorating the pool! Where flags are available they must be considered as much an integral aspect of the lesson as are floats and pull-buoys, and are in place for each session.

Other factors relating to the organisation of a session
Lifeguards
The situation regarding the provision of an appropriate qualified lifesaver for each session when swimmers are in the water is now better understood. However, there is a temptation for some teachers/coaches to consider that this provision is unnecessary if all the swimmers in the pool at any one time are of competition standard. The requirements for lifesaving apply to all sessions, irrespective of the ability of the swimmer in the water, and every teacher/coach should ensure that an appropriately qualified person is always available on the poolside. This may be the teacher/coach concerned, although, ideally, **a person with no teaching or coaching responsibilities should be used.** Whilst many will consider that the likelihood of competitive swimmers getting into difficulties is remote, consideration must always be given to the possibility arising from, for example, cramp, collisions, and medical ailments such as epilepsy.

Teacher/coach certification
Whilst the need for a qualified lifeguard is generally accepted the same degree of rigour is often not applied in respect of the appointment of teachers/coaches with the qualification necessary to fulfil the duties being asked of them. Whilst the contribution made by the interested parents, etc., cannot be understated (many clubs, for example, would cease to exist without this help) having appropriately qualified personnel is a major contributory factor in the safety of swimmers. There is an increasing trend, nationally, towards qualifications which are very specific, and all organisers of teaching/coaching sessions should strive to ensure

that the people who perform these roles have the appropriate qualification to do so. This not only refers to initial training, but also the on-going continuing professional development (CPD) necessary to ensure continued familiarity with current good practice.

Emergency Action Plan

All teachers/coaches should be familiar with the Emergency Action Plan (EAP) applicable to the environment in which they work. Chapter 5 in *Level 1* of the series dealt with this in detail.

Recording of accidents

The *Reporting of Injuries, Diseases and Dangerous Occurences Regulations,* 1985, (RIDDOR) came into effect in April, 1986. These require injuries, disease and occurrences in specified categories to be notified to the relevant enforcing authority. The responsibility for reporting rests with either the employer, the individual if self-employed, or those in control of work premises. In swimming pools, therefore, the responsibility for the reporting of accidents rests with the management of the facility. This does not remove entirely the responsibility of the individual or the club. Every swimming facility should have a clearly defined policy relating to this type of occurrence and it is the responsibility of the club, teacher/coach to ensure that this policy is known and, when necessary, utilised. Many facilities of this nature require that all accidents, no matter how minor, are reported and recorded, but only those which come into the three main categories detailed in RIDDOR will be officially reported to the appropriate Health and Safety Executive.

Immediate notification, (for leisure and entertainment this will be the environmental health department of the local authority) normally by a phone call, is required for the following:

- any fatal injuries to employees or other people in an accident connected with the business concerned, e.g., swimming pool;
- any major injuries to employees or other people in an accident connected with the business concerned. This should be a comprehensive list and will require details of the type of injury, e.g., broken leg or arm, loss of consciousness due to lack of oxygen, etc.;
- any dangerous occurrences listed in the regulations. These include electrical short circuit or overload causing fire or explosion.

In addition to the immediate response a written report will be required by the enforcing authority within seven days of any notifiable incident (shown above).

Responsibility of the club, teacher/coach

The responsibility for those who hire facilities (public and private) is to ensure that there is a system for the reporting of accidents and that this is followed. If a system does not exist then it is essential to devise one which will meet the needs of the user of the facility in addition to the enforcing authority. It is always important to remember that the full effects of some injuries do not always become apparent immediately and, therefore, it is preferable to adopt a system which records more than might actually be needed. It is always better to be in a position of having too much information than too little.

Influence of the *Children Act*

There is still much confusion nationwide concerning the interpretation and implementation of the *Children Act.* The particular section concerning organisations, such as swimming clubs, relates to parental responsibility for children under the age of eight years. If responsibility is transferred on a regular basis to a third party out of the home for a period of time exceeding two hours in any one day, on more than six occasions in any one year, then that person or organisation must be registered as providing a sessional care facility. In order that neither club nor individual should find themselves in breach of the law and, therefore, liable to the imposition of a fine, the ASA would recommend that clubs, and individual teachers/coaches make contact in writing with the Social Services department of their local authority seeking clarification of the procedures required for registration (should it be necessary).

Insurance liability

It is vital for all individual teachers/coaches and clubs to ensure that they have sufficient insurance to cover the activities which they undertake. On an individual basis it is possible to obtain personal liability insurance through an insurance broker or agent, or through membership of a variety of professional organisations. The Institute of Swimming Teachers and Coaches (ISTC), for example, provides insurance cover for those individuals who are involved in the teaching/coaching of swimming on an individual basis. For those working within a club structure it is essential to ascertain the degree of cover available through the club insurance arrangement, and to take out any further protection which is considered necessary. The Amateur Swimming Association (ASA) will advise all affiliated clubs as the most appropriate steps to take in this respect.

The use of electrical equipment and appliances near swimming pools

The *Health and Safety at Work Act* applies to both public and private pools which are hired out for use by swimming clubs. There are duties on pool operators and on users of electrical equipment to ensure that it does not provide a hazard either to employees or visitors to the premises. The *Electricity at Work Regulations,* 1989, are regularly updated and for detailed information a copy of these regulations can be obtained from the Health and Safety Executive. However, there are a number of general points which will help guide all those utilising electrical equipment in close proximity to a swimming pool:

- all necessary electrical equipment, including portable and transportable, should be kept in a dry area at least 3.5 metres from the poolside and protected via a residual current device (RCD) with a sensitivity of 30 mA;
- equipment which by itself would be situated outside 3.5 metres, but because of trailing cables some parts will be used either in the water or by the poolside, e.g., microphones, loudspeakers, timing equipment, must be specifically designed for the purpose as a fault in the supply equipment situated in the dry area could be impressed on the items which are used in the wet areas with consequent hazards;
- the danger comes not only from the items of apparatus, but also from the trailing cables used to connect equipment to electrical circuits;
- the circuit breakers should have a sensitivity or tripping current of not more than 30 milliamps (30 mA) for each socket outlet. The correct operation of circuit breakers must be checked regularly by pressing test buttons on all occasions before they are to be used with equipment;
- all electrical equipment should be properly mounted and/or supported;
- consult the pool authority/management before connecting up any electrical equipment or apparatus as to its suitability, and to ensure that protection devices are installed and working correctly;
- use equipment which is designed for the purpose, either battery operated or reduced voltage wherever possible. Equipment which is designed for either battery or mains use may constitute a hazard if set up by an unauthorised person;
- avoid long cable runs between equipment and the protected socket or supply source;

- in no circumstances whatsoever should swimmers in the water handle electrical equipment, such as speakers or lighting;
- if in doubt about equipment suitability, obtain professional advice;
- **do not interfere with, or touch electrical equipment if you are not properly trained.**

For further information regarding the use of electrical appliances in or near swimming pools contact the Health and Safety Executive (see "Addresses", Part VII).

Management of swimming equipment

An integral aspect of the successful conduct of any swimming session is the availability of a wide range of teaching/coaching aids. Individuals may have their own opinions regarding the most appropriate type of aid to use, but there can be no disagreement concerning the need to have all equipment close by and easily accessible. For equipment like lane dividers and turning flags this will invariably require negotiation with the pool managers to ensure that it is in place prior to the start of the session. Time devoted to preparing a pool for a lesson or training session is time taken away from actual swimming unless suitable allowance is made. It is essential to ensure that smaller equipment, e.g., floats, pull-buoys, hand paddles, is readily available where required and that there is safe storage. If an individual and/or club is in a situation which necessitates having equipment separate from that utilised by the pool staff, a simple, lockable storage basket will be required.

Effective management of swimming aids

Careful planning is required if swimming aids are to be used in the most effective manner. This will involve:

- careful pre-planning of the lesson/session to ensure that the required swimming aids have been identified and are available;
- negotiation with other pool users – this is necessary when there is a limited amount of equipment shared between a number of potential users. It can be extremely frustrating if all teachers/coaches require the same equipment at the same time;
- ensuring that the swimmers are taught both how to use the swimming aids correctly and the benefits of such use;
- regular checking of swimming aids and the discarding of those which are sufficiently damaged;
- establishing a policy for continuous updating and replacement.

Diving into shallow water from starting blocks

The safety issues relating to the teaching of diving, particularly with regard to the depth of water, were outlined in the *Level 1* publication in this series. However, a logical progression from this, particularly for those swimmers who wish to engage in competitive events, relates to the use of starting blocks.

> "It is the ASA's policy that swimmers should not be permitted to dive from a starting block of a maximum height of 500 mm from the water surface into water of a minimum depth of 0.9 m until they have demonstrated an ability to execute correctly the tasks outlined in the Competitive Start Award (CSA)"

Having mastered the basic plunge dive into deep water (see *Level 1* publication in this series), any swimmer wishing to participate in competitive events will need to develop this dive further to ensure a quicker, more efficient start to a race. This will inevitably include starting from a racing platform (starting block) and, therefore, potentially presents a number of hazards. It is essential that swimmers who wish to enter a competitive event should follow a series of progressive practices which will gradually improve their skill level and, therefore, help to avoid the serious neck and back problems which can result from making contact with the bottom of the pool. Ideally, all competitive starts from blocks should take place at the deep end of the pool but, unfortunately, this is not always possible. Relay takeovers in pools with both ends shallow will necessitate entry into shallow water and great care must be taken to ensure that the appropriate training is given. The process of skill development culminating in a swimmer being able to dive safely from a starting block into shallow water is the same process as that associated with learning any skill. Using the ability to perform a plunge dive as the starting point, the swimmer should be guided through a series of progressive practices with the teacher/coach constantly checking the learner's performance and understanding. **Only when the teacher/coach is satisfied that the particular practice has been mastered should the swimmer be allowed to progress to the next stage.**

The ASA Competitive Start Award (CSA) details a series of progressions which all swimmers should follow before being allowed to dive from a starting block into shallow water. Whilst this cannot guarantee the continued safe entry of all swimmers it does provide a sound basis on which teachers/coaches can build. It is important to remember that a swimmer's ability to execute a safe entry during training cannot guarantee that this level of skill will be replicated under the pressure of competition. This factor needs to be taken into account during the training sessions devoted to this activity. A broad outline for progression would be:

- racing start from the side of the pool and into **deep** water;
- racing start from a starting block and into **deep** water;
- racing start from the side of the pool into shallow water (**minimum** 0.9 m);
- racing start from a starting block and into shallow water.

Overtraining

Unlike many other sports, particularly those involving a high degree of physical contact, medical problems are not particularly common in competitive swimmers. Where injury does occur, however, it is often a result of overtraining and will manifest itself in two distinct, but often connected ways:

- damage to part of the body, usually in the joint, muscle or tendon;
- declining performance.

Overuse injuries

These injuries occur as a result of constant and repetitive use of a particular body part which results in pain of that part. Common examples of overuse injuries in swimming are "strain of the triceps muscle tendon at the elbow (which is responsible for the forceful extension of the elbow during the underwater pull) and strains of the lower back muscles, particularly during Breaststroke and Butterfly swimming. Sprains of the ligaments and capsule of the front of the ankle are also common because of the repeated flapping motion of the ankles in swimming". (Costill D. L., Maglischo E. W. and Richardson A. B., *Swimming,* International Olympic Committee Medical Commission, Blackwells Scientific Publications).

There are many ways of treating injuries depending on the individual circumstances, but in all cases professional medical advice should be sort.

Common injuries

- **shoulder injury** – swimming is predominantly an upper body activity and, therefore, the shoulder is susceptible to overuse injury, particularly if hand paddles are used to any great extent during training.

● **knee injury** – Breaststroke swimmers are particularly susceptible to knee injury through repeated stress at the knee joint.

Remember, if there is any doubt concerning the nature of the injury, or where the injury persists, professional medical advice should be sought.

Psychological effect of overtraining

Overtraining refers to "an unplanned reduction or stagnation of performance over a long period in the specific discipline, caused by overstressing the athlete". (Israel (1980) S/Buhl B., *Die Sportliche Trainierbarkheit in der Pubeszenze,* Korperersiehung 30). There are occasions when this may be due entirely to the physical demands being made upon a swimmer during training, although it is more commonly attributable to a combination of factors. Problems created through mental stress are often more difficult to pinpoint and to treat, but the resultant reduction in performance can be significant. The lay term describing this condition is "staleness", and both the parent and teacher/coach have a role to play in the identification and remedy of the situation.

Examples of symptoms are:

● loss of appetite and subsequent weight loss;
● disturbed sleep patterns;
● general lethargy in the pool and apparent disinterest;
● pale facial complexion and rings around the eyes.

Having identified "staleness" it is important to try and establish the cause of the problem. If this is not entirely due to the physical demands of training it is potentially a complex procedure. Mental stress factors might include:

● problems at school, work, or in the home;
● lack of variety in the training programme;
● lack of confidence in the teacher/coach;
● concern about performance in competition;
● too intensive and too much competition.

It could be argued that problems at school, work or in the home are largely the concern of the swimmers' families, although the teacher/coach may well have an important "intermediary" role to play. Many of the points above, however, are very much within the remit of the teacher/coach and immediate, positive action should be taken. If the problem can be traced to a deep rooted lack of confidence in the teacher/coach then the only acceptable course of action may well be for the swimmer to seek the help of a different person. However, this is not always easy and should only occur after full discussion between the swimmer, teacher/coach and parents. The root of the problem may well be a lack of understanding by the swimmer of the short, medium and long term objectives of the training programme. Alternatively, the teacher/coach may not fully appreciate the aspirations of the swimmer and may be imposing a training programme which does not correspond with the individual's desires and personal objectives. Regular and frequent discussion between the three main parties, i.e., swimmer, teacher/coach and parents, is essential to ensure a full understanding and agreement about shared objectives.

If the "staleness" can be traced to lack of variety in the training programme then this should be relatively easy to modify. It may, however, involve the teacher/coach in actively seeking new ideas, methods and knowledge. Post-qualification in-service training, continuing professional development (CPD), is often neglected by teachers/coaches and opportunities for assimilating new concepts missed. The desire to keep an open mind regarding any new developments should be an integral quality of all teachers/coaches, and private reading, attendance at seminars, coaching clinics, etc., are integral aspects of this process. In addition, teachers/coaches should constantly reflect upon their own performance and review where necessary.

Clinical research has established that prolonged exposure to stress, e.g., competition related, may lead to physical illness such as heart disease, high blood pressure, allergies, and respiratory complaints such as asthma. In addition, it has also been linked to psychological problems such as anxiety, depression and behaviour disorders (Cox (1985), *Stress,* Macmillan). These problems can be particularly acute for young swimmers and was highlighted in the recent training of young athletes (TOYA) study. It has been suggested that stress related problems can be generated by over-zealous or intrusive parents (Ogilvie (1981), *The Child athlete: Psychological implications of participation in sport,* Annals of American Academy Number 445; and Orlieb and Botterill (1974), *Every Kid Can Win,* Nelson-Hall); the excessive demands of the coach (Sage (1978), *Humanistic Psychology and Coaching,* W.S. Straub Movement Publication), or pressure from athletes' peers or team mates.

Prolonged exposure to any of the factors contributing to staleness can eventually lead to "burn out" (Pines and Aronsen (1981), *Burn out: From Tedium to Personal Growth,* Free Press Publications), and they noted that "burn out" is characterised by physical depletion, feelings of helplessness, emotional drain and the development of negative self-concept and negative attitudes towards training, life and other people. Whilst there can be no doubt that training and competition can generate stress related disorders there is no evidence to suggest that those involved in youth sports have a higher risk of emotional disorder than those involved in other evaluation activities such as music or drama. In fact, research (Brown (1978), *The Prescription Exercise for Depression,* Physician and Sports Medicine; and Greist J. H. (1979), *Running as a treatment for depression,* Comprehensive Psychiatry, Number 20) has suggested that physical activity may itself be a significant coping mechanism.

PART IV

PROPULSION IN SWIMMING

Introduction to Part IV

No matter at what level the swimmer performs, from non-swimmer to Olympic champion, travelling efficiently through the water is the result of limb movements providing the propulsion and the body creating as little resistance as possible. A sound understanding of the principles associated with streamlining and propulsion, therefore, is essential to good teaching/coaching. Whilst this topic was introduced in *Level 1* of the series, it is so important that a second, more detailed treatment, is offered here.

Chapter 11

The Biomechanics of Competitive Swimming

Carl Payton

Introduction

In recent years the sport of swimming has become the focus of much scientific research from a variety of perspectives. Innovative coaches have often successfully adopted scientific theories, developed from the experimental results of such research, to enable their swimmers to train and compete more effectively. Exercise physiologists, for example, have shown us how blood lactate measurements can be used to determine optimal training intensities and also monitor a swimmer's training status. Sports psychologists have developed strategies designed to bring the swimmer to an optimal state of arousal prior to a race. Competitive swimming has also recently become the subject of much research from another scientific perspective, that of biomechanics.

Biomechanics has been defined as *the study of the structure and function of biological systems by means of the methods of mechanics.* (Hatze H., (1974) *The Meaning of the term "Biomechanics",* Journal of Biomechanics, Number 7, 1974). A biomechanical study of swimming may involve an analysis of the forces acting on and within the swimmer's body – a **kinetic** analysis. Alternatively, the analysis may concentrate on the movement patterns of the swimmer's body (resulting from these forces) – a **kinematic** analysis.

Although some biomechanical research has been criticised for having no immediate relevance to the practising coach, many biomechanists have sought to answer practical, pertinent questions such as, "Which is the fastest starting technique?" "Does shaving-down reduce drag?" "Does the Front Crawl leg kick provide any propulsion?" "What causes sore knees in Breaststroke?"

To optimise performance and minimise the risk of injury, swimming techniques should always be based on sound mechanical principles. Biomechanics enables the teacher/coach to make objective decisions concerning a swimmer's stroke mechanics such as what aspects are correct and incorrect, important and unimportant, efficient and inefficient. A basic knowledge of biomechanics is, therefore, an essential tool to the serious swimming teacher/coach.

Basic biomechanical concepts

Forces – the most fundamental mechanical concept underpinning any sporting skill, including swimming, is that of **Force.** Simply stated, a force is a push (or a pull) that changes, or tries to change, the state of motion of the body on which it acts. To define fully a force, its magnitude, direction and point of application on the body must be given.

In swimming we distinguish between **internal** forces, i.e., those generated within the swimmer's body, for example, a contracting muscle exerting a force on the bones to which it attaches, and **external** forces, those forces exerted on the swimmer by the environment. It is important to realise that although internal forces allow the swimmer to change the position of individual limbs and interact with the environment, it is the external forces resulting from this interaction that actually determine the movements of the swimmer's body as a whole.

It is pertinent therefore to outline all of the external forces encountered by a swimmer during a race. These can be illustrated by way of a free body diagram (Fig 11.1).

● **Body Weight** (W) – this force is due to the gravitational pull of the earth on the swimmer and, therefore, does not change when a swimmer is in the water (contrary to popular belief). Body Weight acts directly downward through the swimmer's **centre of gravity** which is the point in the body about which the weight is evenly distributed.

Figure 11.1 External forces encountered by a swimmer

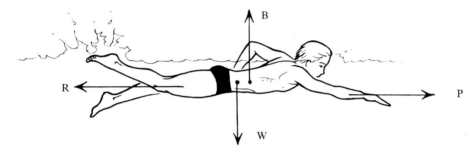

● **Ground Reaction Force** (GRF) – this force acts whenever the swimmer's feet and/or hands are in contact with pool wall or blocks. Its magnitude is exactly equal to that of the force applied to the blocks or pool wall by the swimmer and its direction opposes the force exerted by the swimmer as illustrated in Figure 11.2.

Figure 11.2 Ground reaction force   Force exerted on swimmer by the
                                        starting block – the ground reaction force.

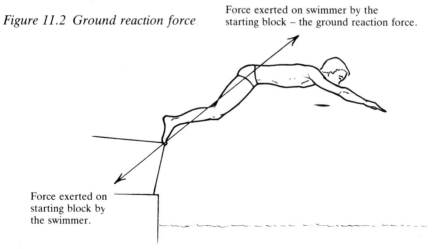

Force exerted on
starting block by
the swimmer.

The execution of skilled racing starts and turns involves the generation of large, sustained and correctly directed ground reaction forces. Starting techniques which incorporate an exaggerated arm swing, e.g., circular backswing start, can generate greater ground reaction forces and, consequently, higher take-off speeds, than those that do not, e.g., Grab start. Unfortunately, considerably more time has to be spent on the starting block generating these larger forces. Nevertheless, swing starts should always be used in relay take overs since the armswing can be initiated before the incoming swimmer touches.

● **Buoyancy Force** (B) – once the swimmer enters the pool an additional force becomes apparent. This force acts vertically upwards through the swimmer's **centre of buoyancy** that is, the centre of volume of the submerged part of the swimmer (Fig. 11.1). The magnitude of the buoyancy force is equal to the weight of water displaced by the swimmer's body (Archimedes' principle). Consequently, if the weight of water displaced by a swimmer is greater than or equal to his body weight, he will float. However, if when fully submerged the weight of water displaced by the swimmer is less than body weight, he will sink.

A swimmer will float, when stationary in the water, if the average body density is less than the density of the water. Although the ability to float may allow a swimmer to ride marginally higher in the water, the importance of floatation should not be overstated. Many world class swimmers are non-floaters. Any additional upthrust required by the swimmer is automatically provided by fluid dynamic forces as the swimmer propels himself through the water.

● **Fluid Dynamic Forces** – these are the forces that the water exerts on the swimmer's body in reaction to the movements he or she makes and are consequently those over which the swimmer has most influence. Since swimming performance is reliant on the effective utilisation of fluid dynamic forces, they will be covered in greater detail in the following section.

Fluid dynamic forces acting in the direction of the swim are termed **propulsive** (P) forces; those opposing the direction of the swim being termed **resistive** (R) forces. These forces can also act perpendicular to the swim direction, in which case they can cause lateral or vertical displacement of the swimmer's body which may have a beneficial or detrimental effect on performance.

To objectively examine how each of these external forces relates to a swimmer's performance requires an understanding of the three laws of motion formulated by Sir Isaac Newton (1642-1727).

Newton's Laws of Motion
● First Law (Law of inertia)
A swimmer will remain stationary, or move with a constant speed (in a straight line), unless acted upon by external forces which are not in equilibrium.

From this law we can conclude that all of the external forces acting on a stationary swimmer waiting for the starter's gun must be in equilibrium, i.e., the ground reaction force must cancel out the weight force. Also, in the flight phase of a racing dive, the horizontal speed of the swimmer remains constant as there are no horizontal forces acting during this period (the effects of air resistance are negligible here).

● Second Law (Law of acceleration)
(For bodies whose mass remain constant throughout the motion, e.g., a swimmer's body).

When the external forces acting on a swimmer are not in equilibrium, the swimmer will accelerate in the direction of the resultant (net) force. The resulting acceleration is proportional to the net force acting on the swimmer. This law is often stated in the form of the following equation:

$$\text{Force (net)} = \text{Mass} \times \text{Acceleration}$$

At any instant within a stroke cycle a swimmer is subject to resistive forces (R) which have to be offset by the generation of propulsive forces (P). Newton's second law shows that:

If P>R the swimmer will accelerate, e.g., leg thrust in the Breaststroke kick.

insweep in the arms in the Butterfly.

If P<R the swimmer will decelerate, e.g., leg recovery in the Breaststroke kick.

recovery of the arms in the Butterfly.

If P=R then no net force is acting on the swimmer horizontally and no acceleration will take place, that is, the swimmer's velocity will remain constant.

● Third Law (Law of interaction)

For every action (force) exerted by the swimmer on a second body, there will be a reaction (force) equal in magnitude but opposite in direction exerted by the second body on the swimmer.

Thus, when a swimmer exerts a downwards and backwards force on a starting block, the block applies a (ground reaction) force of equal magnitude on the swimmer, but in an upwards and forwards direction (Fig. 11.2). Similarly, if a swimmer applies a force to a mass of water, an equal force is received by the swimmer from the water.

Summary

Swimmers regardless of the technique being used, must generate propulsive forces **in excess** of the resistive forces acting if they are to accelerate **within a stroke cycle.** Improved acceleration can be achieved by either increasing the propulsive force produced or decreasing the resistive forces acting at a given instant within cycle (the effect is the same). It follows, therefore, that swimmers should always strive for a continuous application of propulsive force throughout each stroke cycle to offset the ever-present resistive forces. This can easily be achieved provided catch-up timing (Front Crawl and Back Crawl) and excessive gliding (Breaststroke) are avoided.

Although, during certain phases within each stroke cycle, the resistive forces will inevitably exceed the propulsive forces, the deceleration that results will be minimised if the swimmer continually seeks to maximise the propulsive forces, and minimise the resistive forces, acting on his body. To be able to do this, a general understanding of how these forces are generated and the factors that affect their magnitude is essential.

Propulsive and resistive forces

Propulsive forces in swimming

Within each competitive swimming stroke, teachers/coaches and swimmers are constantly seeking the combination of arm and leg actions which will most effectively produce large and sustained propulsive forces. An understanding of the basic fluid mechanics of propulsion is vitally important to the coach and swimmer as it will ultimately dictate the manner in which the strokes are taught and swum.

The exact mechanism by which propulsive forces are generated has long been a topic of debate amongst swimmers, coaches and sports scientists. A number of propulsive theories have been proposed the first being the **propulsive drag theory** which was widely accepted for decades up until the early 1970s. Based on Newton's law of Interaction, this theory suggests that swimmers use their hands as paddles and gain propulsion by pulling and pushing them directly backwards through the water. It argues that the forwardly directed reaction force, resulting from the drag on the hand, is the source of propulsion. (Fig. 11.3)

Figure 11.3 The propulsive drag theory

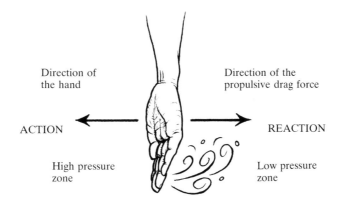

This theory also claims that the horizontal components of the downward and backward and upward and backward movements of the feet in the Butterfly, Back Crawl and Front Crawl evoke a forward directed (and, therefore, propulsive) reaction force from the water. Although swimmers could theoretically obtain all of their propulsion from drag forces, it is inconceivable that competitive swimmers do so since drag is a very inefficient source of propulsion (as illustrated by the "doggie", or Front paddle, which relies on drag propulsion!).

If, as the theory suggests, the hands are used as paddles to push water backwards, at the commencement of the stroke the water immediately behind the hand will naturally accelerate. For the remainder of the stroke cycle the swimmer is then confronted with the problem of trying to continue to exert a large force against a mass of water that is rapidly moving away from him. Maintaining propulsion using hydrodynamic drag is thus not easy and is analogous to an athlete attempting to gain propulsive forces whilst running on marbles!

In 1970 Dr James Counsilman, the highly respected American Coach, reported that the paths followed by the hands of elite swimmers did not follow a straight-line but, in fact, involved significant **vertical** and **lateral** sculling motions. In addition he observed that, contrary to drag theory, the swimmers' hands did not move appreciably backwards in the water but appeared stationary as the swimmer's body moved over them. Based on this evidence, the **propulsive lift theory** was presented at the First International Symposium on Biomechanics in Swimming in Brussels in 1970, where it was suggested that competitive swimmers use their hands (and the feet in Breaststroke) not as paddles, but also as **hydrofoils,** and that some of their propulsion comes from hydrodynamic lift forces generated through lateral and vertical sculling movements.

Lift forces

Lift forces can be generated when a body part moving through the water is shaped to resemble that of a foil (Fig. 11.4).

Figure 11.4 Lift forces

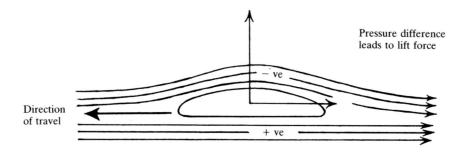

As the foil is moved through the water the fluid separates at the front edge. The fluid that travels over the curved upper surface reaches the rear edge of the foil at the same time as the fluid passing over the flat underside. Thus the fluid on the curved side is forced to travel at a greater speed than that underneath (as it has further to travel in the same time).

The Italian scientist, Bernoulli, discovered that wherever the speed of flow of a fluid is forced to increase, the pressure exerted by that fluid is reduced. Thus, in Fig. 11.4, the pressure exerted by the water on the top of the foil is less than that exerted on the underside. This inbalance in pressures across the foil (pressure differential) results in a lift force directed perpendicular to the direction of movement of the foil.

A cross-sectional view of a swimmer's hand when slightly cupped shows it to resemble a foil shape, thus, when a swimmer slices the hand through water, a lift force is generated perpendicular to the direction of the hand's movement (Fig. 11.5).

Figure 11.5 Swimmer's hand, slightly cupped

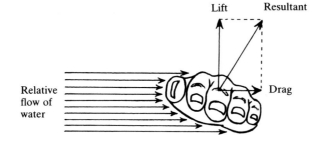

Figure 11.6 Swimmer treading water, sculling hands in a horizontal plane

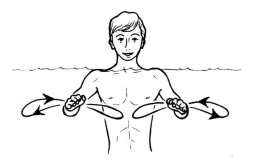

Figure 11.7 Hand sweeping outward and downward in a vertical plane

Consequently, if the hands are sculled in a horizontal plane, e.g., when treading water, the lift force acts vertically (Fig. 11.6). Alternatively, if the hands are sculled in a vertical plane, like a boat propellor, the lift forces act horizontally (Fig. 11.7) and, by definition, are propulsive in nature. Vertical and lateral sculling actions are thus vitally important to the competitive swimmer.

It is important to note that sculling movements result in hydrodynamic lift and drag forces acting on the **hand** (not the body) of the swimmer. **These forces are, therefore, not directly responsible for propelling the body, they simply enable the hand to be fixed in the water while the swimmer pulls the body past the hand.** Swimmers often get the impression that they are pulling and pushing the hand through the water when in fact, they are merely pulling and pushing the hand along their body.

The magnitude of the lift forces generated by a swimmer depends on:

- the speed of the hand through the water;
- the size and shape of the hand (research suggests the hand should be slightly cupped with the fingers together to maximise lift forces);
- the angle of attack of the hand.

Angle of attack

This is defined as the angle at which the hand is inclined to the relative fluid flow, that is, the angle between the palm of the hand and its direction of movement (Fig. 11.8(a) 11.8(b) 11.8(c) on page 122).

Figure 11.8 Angle of attack

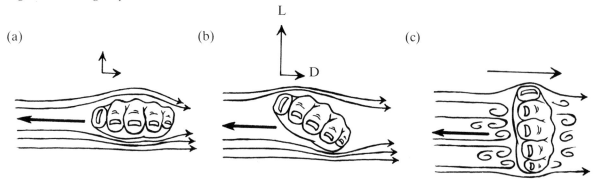

As the angle of attack is increased, the pressure differential, and thus the lift force, also increases. The amount of form drag also increases due to the greater amount of surface area exposed to the flow. Research suggests that lift forces are most effectively generated with angles of attack between 15 and 55 degress. The lift forces rapidly diminish at attack angles higher than this until purely a drag force is acting (compare Figs. 11.8(c) and 11.3).

For any given hand position, the total force acting on the hand can be considered to be the sum of the lift and drag forces acting at that instant. A combination of lift and drag forces act throughout a stroke cycle and their relative contributions depend on the stroke performed and the phase within the stroke, for example, lift forces dominate throughout the Breaststroke, whereas in the Front Crawl, lift forces dominate during the downsweep with drag forces providing most of the propulsion during the insweep.

Propulsive forces from kicking

The swimmer's feet can also be used as propellors to provide lift forces for propulsion. This is most evident in the Breaststroke kick where, contrary to popular belief, the feet do not travel backward appreciably in the water. Rather, they sweep outward, downward and inward describing a circular path in a vertical plane thus generating forwardly directed lift forces. Teachers/coaches and swimmers should, therefore, place the emphasis on the circling of the feet during the kick rather than on thrusting them backwards.

The contribution to the total propulsive force made by the Front Crawl and Back Crawl flutter kick and the dolphin kick of the Butterfly is considerably less than that made by Breaststroke kick. The position and movement paths of the feet associated with these kicks are not as conducive to lift force generation, and it is likely that drag forces play a greater role here. Some researchers and teachers/coaches have even argued that these kicking actions make no direct contribution to propulsion but serve to stabilise the body and maintain horizontal alignment thus reducing the resistive force acting.

Summary

Not only must swimmers learn the correct pulling and kicking patterns, they must also develop a "feel" for the water flow over their hands and feet. They must constantly adjust the pitch of their hands and feet throughout the propulsive phases of each stroke in order to optimise the resultant of the lift and drag forces acting on them.

Resistive force in swimming

These are the forces that retard the motion of the swimmer through the water and should be minimised at all times. Resistive forces are sometimes termed **drag forces,** since they act in the opposite direction to the movement of the swimmer's body or body part. The previous section illustrated that drag forces which can be utilised for propulsion, the drag forces discussed here are resistive.

Viscous drag

As the swimmer moves through the water, the layer of fluid adjacent to the body is slowed down by the frictional forces exerted on it. This layer in turn exerts a frictional force on the layer of fluid next to it slowing it down, and so on. The region of water surrounding the swimmer's body affected in this way is termed the **boundary layer.** The forwardly directed force exerted by the swimmer to create the boundary layer results in the water exerting an equal, but backwardly directed, force on the swimmer; this force is termed the **viscous drag** or **skin friction.**

The magnitude of the viscous drag is determined by, amongst other things, the roughness of the swimmer's body, consequently swimmers wear tight-fitting costumes composed of smooth fabric, e.g., lycra and swimming caps, to reduce this form of resistance. Although male swimmers often shave their body hair to further reduce viscous drag, there has not yet been any convincing research to indicate that this practice reduces drag by a measurable amount. Viscous drag makes only a very small contribution to the overall resistive force acting on the swimmer.

Form drag

This is the major contributor to the overall resistive force experienced by the swimmer and, as the name suggests, depends on the form or shape of the swimmer's body. As the swimmer moves through the water, the water particles in front of the body meet it head-on forming a zone of relatively high water pressure. As the water passes around the body a pocket of turbulence is developed behind the body and a zone of relatively low water pressure is created (Fig. 11.9). The imbalance in water pressure in front of and behind the swimmer results in a pressure differential being created. Where such a pressure differential exists, a force is directed from high to low pressure, i.e., opposes the direction of motion. This force is termed the **form drag.** Notably, this source of drag increases approximately with the square of the speed of the swimmer, that is, if the swimmer doubles his speed, the form drag needed to be overcome is quadrupled.

Figure 11.9 Form drag

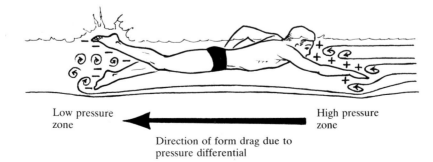

Low pressure zone

High pressure zone

Direction of form drag due to pressure differential

123

Several factors affect the magnitude of form drag including the frontal (cross-sectional) area of the swimmer presented to the water, and the shape of the body in the water. Form drag can be minimised by good streamlining. This is achieved by maintaining good horizontal body alignment with the shoulders, hips and feet near the surface of the water. Not only does this reduce the frontal area presented to the water but also narrows the low pressure wake behind the swimmer. Form drag can also be minimised in the Front Crawl and Back Crawl by avoiding excessive lateral motions of the body. These may be the result of wide swinging arm recoveries or fluid dynamic forces inadvertently directed laterally rather than forwards.

Modern Breaststroke swimmers tend to recover their hands, shoulders and chest over the water, reducing the frontal area being pushed through the water, thus lowering the form drag. Additionally, many now **drop** their hips during the recovery of the legs. This manoeuvre may actually reduce the form drag encountered at this stage in the stroke since it allows the legs to be recovered with much less hip flexion, that is, less forward motion of the thighs. This results in the thighs presenting a sloping relatively streamlined surface to the water. Failure to drop the hips during leg recovery results in the thighs having to be pushed downward and forward 'square-on' to the water increasing form drag.

Wave drag

This component of the drag force acts at the air-water interface and makes a significant contribution to the overall drag experienced by the swimmer. When a swimmer moves a body part at the water's surface, e.g., hand entry in the Back Crawl, a wave is created. The reaction force that the wave exerts on the swimmer constitutes the wave drag. The magnitude of the wave drag increases with greater vertical movements of the swimmer and also increases with swimming speed (reflected by the higher bow wave in front of the swimmer).

At a given swimming speed skilled swimmers have been shown to produce smaller waves than less-skilled swimmers and, therefore, experience less wave drag. Unlike form drag, this source of resistance increases in proportion to the cube of the swimmer's speed, thus doubling swimming speed increases wave drag by a factor of eight! Swimmers can reduce wave drag by avoiding unnecessary, vertical motions of limbs (or the body as a whole) at the water's surface. For example, excessive lifting of the head during the breathing in Butterfly, or slapping the back of the hand onto the water in the Back Crawl arm entry.

Summary

Competitive swimmers must use swimming techniques that minimise resistive forces if they hope to get maximum benefit from the propulsive forces they develop. The importance of reducing form drag by good streamlining cannot be over-emphasised. This applies not only during swimming but also during the glides phase of starts and turns. The formation of waves can severely retard a swimmer's progress and excessive vertical and lateral body movements and splashing should be avoided where possible. Although of relatively minor importance, the effect of viscous drag should not be ignored. The use of close-fitting, lightweight swim suits and swimming caps is recommended since they can only enhance (not inhibit) a swimmer's performance.

Chapter 12

Sculling

Jennifer Gray

Introduction

Sculling is a method of creating either propulsion or height in the water and consists of moving the hands in such manner that continuous pressure is produced. During all sculling actions the hands move away from and towards the centre line of the body; there is no recovery phase to the action. Scooping or finning actions are often taught, but these should not be confused with sculling because there is a backward and forward element and, therefore, a recovery phase. These latter actions do not produce continuous propulsion. Whilst sculling is most efficiently utilised by the synchronised swimmer, it is also an integral part of all swimming strokes.

The theory of sculling is based on Bernoulli's theory. This is discussed in detail in the previous chapter. There is also an introduction to the topic in *Level 1* of the series. The above references also deal with the associated issues of "angle of attack" and "pitch". The latter is related to the "feel" of the water, the kinaesthetic sense which distinguishes the talented from the less talented performer. All swimming strokes are analysed into insweeps and outsweeps, and to create maximum lift throughout the stroke the pitch of the hand is constantly changing. This allows maximum purchase on the water throughout the stroke pathway.

In all sculling actions the speed at which the hand moves is also vital to gaining maximum propulsion (lift). Too great a speed results in slippage through the water. Too little speed gives reduced propulsion and is often the result of the swimmer's lack of strength. It is not sufficient to ask the swimmers just to 'feel' or 'get hold of' the water. Sculling should be an integral part of swimming teaching/coaching as well as a specialised skill required by the synchronised swimmer. It is through the teaching of sculling that the competitive swimmer will learn to 'feel' the water and be able to pitch the hand correctly throughout the stroke.

The basic sculling action

It is always more beneficial to practise the sculling action in the water as it is important to get the 'feel' of the movement and the effect that the hands are having. However, sometimes it is necessary to bring the swimmers onto land to correct faulty sculling actions.

Basic practices

- the swimmer stands in shoulder depth water with the arms out stretched parallel to, and just under, the water surface (Fig. 12.1(a)). The hands must be palms down, slightly curved, firm with the fingers together. Starting with the thumbs touching, the hands angle outwards to approximately 45 degrees and then move away from each other. The hands move to a position just outside the line of the shoulders (Fig. 12.1(b)). From this position, the hands rotate inwards, again at an angle of approximately 45 degrees, and then the arms move to their original position. Gradually the tempo is increased. Care must be taken to ensure that the pitch of the hands is changed before the arms move on their new pathway. This practice should be continued until the swimmer can feel the increased pressure under the hands.

Figure 12.1(a) and (b) Basic practices

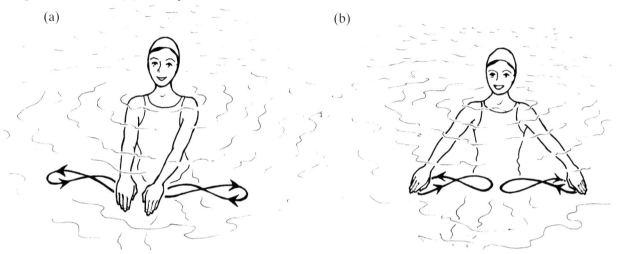

- the swimmer starts close to and facing the pool side, arms resting on the pool side palms down (Fig. 12.2(a)). The arms start close together. On the outsweep the hands rotate so that the thumbs brush along the top of the pool side (Fig. 12.2(b)). On the insweeps, the palms rotate inwards so that the little fingers brush the side (Fig. 12.2(c)). Again, it is important that the turn of the hands is completed at the extremities of each movement and care should be taken to ensure that the angle of tilt does not exceed 45 degrees. This practice is particularly useful for swimmers who have difficulty in obtaining the timing of the change of pitch.

Figure 12.2(a), (b) and (c) Basic practices continued

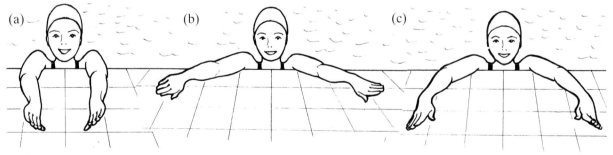

- the swimmer adopts a back lying position with the feet resting on the rail or trough (Fig. 12.3(a)) or, if neither of these are available, a partner may be used to support the feet. The swimmer practices the sculling action with the hands close by the sides of the hips. The hands should be deep enough so as not to disturb the water surface (Fig. 12.3(b)).

● the swimmer practices the previous sculling action without support. To stop the legs sinking, the swimmer should tighten the muscles at the front of the thighs. Swimmers with heavily muscled legs may need pull buoys for support.

Figure 12.3(a) and (b) Basic practices in the horizontal position

(a)

(b)

This basic sculling action (flat scull) produces only uplift and not propulsion. To produce head first movement (standard scull), the hands are tilted away from the swimmer. The swimmer starts as for the first basic sculling practice with the arms just under and parallel to the surface of the water. The upward tilt from the wrists is approximately 45 degrees, but this depends on the wrist flexibility of the individual swimmer. The arms remain straight. In maintaining the 45 degrees tilt the arms perform the same sculling action. The swimmer will soon find it difficult to keep the feet on the bottom of the pool and will start to move backwards. Once movement has been produced the swimmer lies back in the water, presses the hands down to a position beside the hips and moves head first. The body should be as flat and streamlined as possible.

Feet first movements (reverse scull) are produced by altering the angle at the wrist so that the fingers point at an angle of approximately 45 degrees towards the bottom of the pool. The same basic sculling action is used. Movement using this scull is comparatively slow.

Major teaching points:
● scull with straight elbows;
● scull from the shoulders;
● keep the hands below the surface of the water. Try not to disturb the surface;
● keep the movement smooth and continuous;
● keep the hands very slightly cupped;
● fingers together;
● firm wrists;
● maintain a constant angle at the wrist;

- maximum tilt of 45 degrees;
- reverse the angle of tilt at the end of each sweep.

Major faults

- feet sinking – the swimmer should pull in tight on the front of the thighs. 'Feel as though the knee caps are being pulled into the costume' – this will shorten the fronts of the legs and so lift the feet. Pull buoys or floats may be used for added support. Performing the sculling action while gently fluttering kicking will also help.
- travelling sideways – one hand may be lower in the water than the other. The swimmer moves towards the deeper hand. Alternatively, one hand may be pressing out more than the other. The swimmer moves away from the dominant hand.
- erratic travel – possibly elbows bent. Hand action forwards and backwards rather than sideways. Reteach the basic sculling action standing in shallow water. Ensure that the elbows are straight.
- lack of travel – may be lack of upward tilt of the hands from the wrists. Perform the sculling action with the arms resting on the top of the pool side. Ensure that the palms are raised from the side.
- lack of travel – possibly lack of angle of pitch. Perform the sculling action whilst standing in the shallow end. Try to create whirl pools above the hands.

Fun activities using sculling

In all sculling games and competitions, the teacher/coach should ensure that sculling actions are being used. Faster body movement will usually be achieved by using scooping, finning or Breaststroke actions, but these do not aid the production of good sculling techniques:

- **sculling to counts or music** – the teacher/coach gives a number of counts/beats for the swimmer to travel in a given direction. The swimmer changes as directed. Changes should occur with the changes in the phrasing of the music;
- **distance races** – great care must be taken to ensure that the correct technique is used;
- **partner races** – one swimmer places the feet around the chin of the other swimmer. The swimmers then travel over a given distance. More than two swimmers can join in a similar manner:
  - the swimmers start with a partner in the middle of the pool. They join ankles and try to pull or push their partner across the pool;
  - one of the pair adopts a sitting or tub position in the water. The partner joins feet around the neck and then pushes or pulls the partner across the width;
- **whirl pools** – the swimmers try to create whirl pools above their hands.

Sculling variations

Once the three basic sculling actions have been mastered, a variety of other sculls using the same techniques can be learned.

Sculls using the standard hand position
Torpedo Scull (Feet first travel)
The swimmer adopts a flat, back laying (supine) position with the hands extended beyond the head. The arms must be deep enough so they can scull underwater. The wrists are hyperextended so that the fingers

point towards the bottom of the pool. The elbows remain straight and the sculling action is narrow with the arms moving just outside the line of the shoulders. On the outward sweep, the palms press outwards and on the inward sweep, they press towards each other. The angle of pitch in both directions should be 45 degrees.

Canoe Scull (Head first travel)
The swimmer is in the prone position, with the back arched so the heels are at the surface and the chin is resting on the surface. The face is dry. The body tension is held throughout the scull. The arms are extended along the side of the body and they scull away from and towards the hips.

Lobster Scull (Head first travel)
The swimmer adopts a prone position with the face in or out of the water. It is easier to maintain a streamlined position with the face in the water. The arms are extended in front of the swimmer at an angle up to 45 degrees to the water surface. The exact angle will depend on the buoyancy of the swimmer.

Sculls using the reverse hand position
Dolphin scull/Reverse torpedo (Head first travel)
This scull is known by either name and is the reverse action to the torpedo scull. It is now also commonly known as dolphin scull as it is used in Sychronised Swimming to start the dolphin figure. The swimmer is supine with the arms extended beyond the head. The wrists are flexed so that the fingers are towards the water surface. The arms must be deep enough to allow the fingertips to be under water. Head first progression using this scull is usually quite slow.

Reverse lobster/Alligator scull (Head first travel)
"Alligator scull" is the American name for this scull. It is a most appropriate name as the swimmer travels head first in the water with the eyes just peeping above the surface. The swimmer adopts the prone position with the body very tight and streamlined. The arms are in front of the body at an angle appropriate to support the weight of the swimmer. The less buoyant the swimmer the deeper the hands should be. The wrists are flexed with the fingers at an angle of about 45 degrees towards the bottom of the pool.

Sculls using the flat hand position (No travel)
Support scull
This scull is used in Synchronised Swimming whenever the swimmer is inverted in the water. It is a difficult scull to master but is the key to becoming a good synchronised swimmer. The elbows are flexed and held into the sides of the swimmer; the forearms are parallel to the water surface. The upper arms remain relatively stationary and the lower arms move away from and towards the centre line of the body. On the outward scull, the wrists rotate so the palms face away from each other and on the inward scull they are at a 45 degree angle towards each other. The rotation on the outward movement is very difficult and requires practice. However, the rotation on the inward movement occurs quite naturally and great care should be taken to insure the 45 degree angle is not exceeded. The movement is best practised in a standing position in shallow water. When the sculling pattern is established, the swimmer can progress to travelling feet first in a prone position or hanging from the pool side by the back of the legs and practising the movement in an inverted position (See Fig. 12.4(a) and 12.4(b) overleaf). Eventually, the swimmer can practise holding various body shapes only using support scull, e.g., (See Fig. 12.5(a) and 12.5(b) overleaf).

Figure 12.4(a) and (b) Support sculls

(a)

(b)

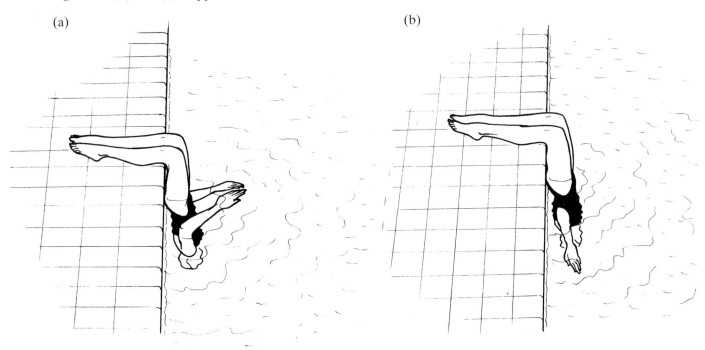

Figure 12.5(a) and (b) Holding shapes

(a)

(b)

PART V

THE STRUCTURE OF THE COMPETITIVE SCENE

Introduction to Part V

There seems little point in being in the business of improving the quality of learners' performances in any sphere of life, and at any level, if, at the same time, there is no knowledge or understanding of the opportunities open to those learners as they improve. Part V sets out the opportunities so that teachers/coaches can contribute to their swimmers' background by giving them more information upon which to base their swimming "career" decisions.

Chapter 13

Swimming Clubs and the Competition Scene

Trevor Thomas

The Competition Ladder

A club with a well motivated teaching/coaching staff and a well balanced learn to swim programme will produce competent swimmers who will want to test their skill levels against other swimmers. This can be done through the ASA Awards schemes or by taking part in competition at the most appropriate level. The use of ASA Awards to compare levels of competence can sometimes have its limitations and competition can often offer a greater range of options.

Where there is an existing well established club which combines learning to swim with a teaching/coaching development programme the structure for competition will already be in place. In the case of a new club in a new pool, or a club that previously saw its role as mainly social, or having a strong bias towards the young beginner and the testing for ASA Awards, there may be less expertise available. Where suitable facilities exist, such a club might wish to include some competitive swimming in its programme. The first and easiest step is to organise and stage a club gala. This can be tailored to suit the level of ability of its members, the numbers to be catered for and the time available. This type of event can be part of, or take the place of, one of the club night sessions. This club gala can include races across the width for the young learner/novice and along the length(s) for the more able. The events should be well within the capability of the swimmers and the taking part should be an enjoyable experience.

The rewards for success at this level need special consideration. The achievement must be acknowledged and a simple award of a certificate or pennant bearing a record of the achievement should suffice. The road to the Olympics is a long one involving a lot of hard work, with many more rostrums to climb before reaching a realistic, ultimate goal. The ultimate goal, of course, is based on the individual's aspirations and abilities but, whatever the level, it is earned by a disciplined commitment to achieving success. This is brought about through competition at many levels, each stage being harder and tougher than the previous one and demanding a higher degree of commitment to achieving greater skills, stamina and endurance. The stages of competition from the club gala to the highest level of excellence will involve the learning of many strokes at several distances before the best combination to achieve success and recognition is found.

Competition and ASA law

In England ASA law governs competitive swimming for all affiliated clubs. Teachers/coaches should have an *ASA Handbook,* an annual publication, which includes a logical and easily followed index of topics which refer to specific laws related to competition. The competitive events are swum using the following strokes: Backstroke, Breaststroke, Butterfly, Freestyle. The reader will note that the terms Back Crawl and Front Crawl are not used to describe competitive events held under the laws of the ASA or FINA (Fédération de Natation Internationale Amateur). In individual medley events, the strokes are swum in the following order: Butterfly, Backstroke, Breaststroke, Freestyle. Whilst in medley relay events, each leg is swum in the order of Backstroke, Breaststroke, Butterfly, Freestyle. It should also be remembered that the sport as a whole consists of four disciplines, Swimming, Diving, Water Polo and Synchronised Swimming. Each discipline has its own Technical Committee, laws, conditions and teaching/coaching certificates. This chapter is biased towards the discipline of 'speed' Swimming.

Distances and events used in major competition

The distances for men and women for the Backstroke, Breaststroke and Butterfly events, are 50 metres, 100 metres and 200 metres, whilst the distances in Freestyle events are 50 metres, 100 metres, 200 metres, 400 metres, 800 metres (Female) and 1500 metres (Male). Individual Medley events are 200 metres (4 × 50m) and 400 metres (4 × 100m), the Freestyle Team events are 4 × 100 metres and 4 × 200 metres (Women only compete in this event at World Championship level) and the Medley Team event is 4 × 100 metres. The above strokes and distances will be used for FINA swimming events, namely, the Olympic Games, World Championships, FINA World Cup, Area Games, e.g., the European Championships, and international contests between countries affiliated to FINA. The above strokes and distances will also be used at the ASA national championships and competitions and in the championships and competitions of the ASA districts.

The dates and format for the domestic competitions will follow a pattern initiated by the date and location of major swimming events that are under the control of FINA or LEN (Ligue Europeene de Natation), which follow a four year cycle:

Year 1 – Olympic Games (FINA) every four years
Year 2 – European Swimming Championships (LEN) every two years
Year 3 – World Swimming Championships (FINA) every four years
Year 4 – European Swimming Championships (LEN) every two years.

England, together with Scotland and Wales, will compete in all these events as part of the Amateur Swimming Federation of Great Britain (ASFGB) Team.

After these major events of the year have been established the dates of the domestic championships are then decided. The ASA championships are set to coincide with the closing date for entries for a particular major event and could be used as the trials for team selection, although separate 'trials' are sometimes held if the Olympic Games or the World Championships are held in the Southern Hemisphere.

When the dates of ASA events have been set, the five districts of the ASA arrange the dates of their own championships and competitions so that qualifying times achieved at these events can reach the ASA Office before the closing date set for entry to the "Nationals". Similarly, the majority of county championships and competitions dates will have been set so that qualifying times achieved at these events can reach the Swimming Secretary of the appropriate district before the closing date.

The Esso National Age Group Competition individual events will be swum in single year age groups for heats and finals, 12, 13, 14, 15, 16, 17 years of age. For team events the age groups will be 11/12 years, 13/14 years, 15/16 years. In the ASA districts Esso Age Group Individual events will also be an 11 years of age group. It is always advisable to check the schedule of events for district competitions. There are some variations to be found between the Age Group programmes of the county associations.

Entry to the ASA national, district (counties) and open competition is by completing an entry form which must contain the entrant's name and ASA registration number, to prove that s/he is an eligible competitor, the name of the club of which s/he is a member, and to sign an acceptance of the promoter's conditions. More detailed information is to be found in the General Competition Laws section of the *ASA Handbook*. The handbooks of the ASA, the five districts and their county associations will all list the conditions required for their own particular championships and competitions, and will also give the dates, venues and qualifying times required for each event.

Levels of competition available

The next stage above the club gala could be an inter club 'friendly', which could be a contest between two clubs of similar strength, with an agreed programme of the strokes and distances to be swum. This could then develop into a contest where three or more clubs are invited to fill the remaining lanes in the pool. It can, however, be very useful to have a spare lane in this type of gala allowing space for the reserves, who might otherwise not have an opportunity to swim. At many open events, and in minor competitions, the strokes used will be the same as for national events, but a wide variation will be encountered in the distances and programme of events to suit the promoter. Alternative distances could include 25 metre races, for individual events in the four strokes, a 100 metre Individual Medley ($4 \times 25m$) race and for the Freestyle and Medley 100 metres Team Races ($4 \times 25m$). The Freestyle Team Race is sometimes swum using more than 4 swimmers, these are often referred to as 'Cannons'.

At this stage swimming and competition can become a serious matter and those in charge of novice competitions should ensure that pressures are not increased in such a way that improvements are not expected too fast and too soon. ASA competition laws make it illegal for a child of nine, as at 31 December in the year of competition, to compete in any open event advertised as being held under ASA law.

Graded swimming

Introduced in its present form in 1980, Graded Swimming is intended to be an incentive scheme for all swimmers, whether they be swimming as part of a club team in an open event, or in regular time trials organised within the club. The scheme allows all competitors to assess their own standards by comparing their latest times and grades, against those previously recorded and published.

Graded swimming tables

The tables, compiled for the ASA by Graham Sykes, are updated every four years and are based on the changes in World Record times. They cover age groups for boys and girls, 12 years/Under, 13/14 years, 15/16 years and 17 years/Over. The system has four grades which are, National, AA, A and B, and cover all strokes and distances. Everyone below B is automatically a C grade. National grade is approximately the same standard as national championship qualifying time; AA, is about district standard; A, is county standard and B is a good club swimmer. Open Graded Meets are often confined to a grade(s) in the tables.

A brief summary of the ASA laws on racing by children shows that the minimum ages at which a swimmer may take part in a swimming race are as follows:

- events restricted to members of one club   – No minimum age
- open relay races other than in district and national competition   – 9 years
- inter-club events limited to not more than eight clubs which do not form part of a series of events as in a league   – 9 years
- open individual events, other than in district and national   – 10 years
- competitions, relay events in district competitions   – 10 years
- individual events in district competitions   – 11 years

- relay events in national competitions   − 11 years
- individual events in national competitions   − 12 years
- for all categories, the age is that attained in the year of competition

League swimming

Another stage in the development of competition could be the club taking part in a registered 'League'. The 'Junior Leagues' cater for swimmers from nine to twelve years of age. The events for boys and girls are swum in pool lengths of 25 yards, 25 metres, 27½ yards, 33⅓ metres or 36⅔ yards. There are individual events for 11 and 12 year old swimmers over one length of the pool on Backstroke, Breaststroke, Butterfly and Freestyle, and Medley and Freestyle Team races. The nine year olds are restricted to relay events only. There are several leagues which include the 'Speedo National Junior Inter-League Swimming Competition', consisting of 12 leagues organised in regional rounds and which culminate in a national final.

By providing competition between clubs of similar standards, participation in one of the Speedo Swimming Leagues could be ideal since all registered swimmers in a club could be involved. Each of the Speedo Swimming Leagues has several divisions, each providing for promotions and relegations. The big clubs, with a large number of competitive swimmers, are allowed to enter more than one team. New teams in the league system are required to start in the lowest division and have to justify promotion by becoming the champion of that division. All the divisional galas take place monthly and at the same time, in different venues. Some leagues operate in the months of October, November, December and others in the months of January, February, March. The Speedo Swimming League Final takes place in September, with finalists coming from the Division 1 winners from each of the respective leagues.

With slight variations in distances the Speedo Swimming League programme has individual events on all strokes and the Individual Medley, for the 10, 11 years, 13 years and under, 15 years and under and Open age groups, and in Freestyle and Medley Team races for the 9, 10 and 11 years, 13 years and under, 15 years and under and Open age groups. The events are swum in pool lengths from 25 to 50 metres. For pools of 3 lengths to the 100 metres/110 yards, 10, 11 years age group will swim 2 lengths. In 25 metres, 27½ yards, or 50 metre pool, they will swim the number of lengths required to complete 50 metres. All the other age groups will swim the number of lengths required to swim 100 metres/110 yards. For all age groups the Individual Medley will be a 4 × 1 length race. In pools of 3 or 4 lengths to 100 metres/110 yards, the Freestyle Team races distances will be 4 × 1 length for the 9, 10 & 11 years age group, 4 × 2 lengths for the 13 years and under and the 15 years and under age groups. For the Open age group the race will be 6 × 2 lengths. For Medley Team races, distances will be 4 × 2 lengths for the open age group and 4 × 1 length for the other age groups. In 50 metre pools, for the Freestyle Team races, the distances will be 4 × 50 metres for all age groups other than the Open, which will be a 6 × 50 metres race.

Further opportunities for the individual

For the individual swimmer(s) there are many opportunities available to suit any level of competence. These are to be found in Open Competitions, or "Open Meets", and these are extensively advertised in publications such as the *Swimming Times*. This publication carries notices of a wide range of events from those at national level downwards, and in all disciplines of the sport of swimming, i.e., Swimming, Open Masters, Diving, Synchronised Swimming and Water Polo.

Open competitions

An open competition is a competition to which entry is not limited to members of any one club. A promoter may, however, impose other restrictions on entry and clubs and individuals are strongly advised to familiarise themselves with ASA law on these competitions. An inter club contest is not regarded as an open competition if it involves no more than eight clubs, the contest takes place on one occasion, and it is not part of a series, as in a league competition. The promoter can refuse to accept an entry but must, if requested, give reasons for the refusal in writing. An entry form may be returned if the information on it is incorrect. These forms are also governed by General Competition Laws. Teachers/coaches are again reminded that they should familiarise themselves with those laws by referring to a **current** *ASA Handbook*.

Progression through the ASA calendar

● County (or Area) Championships and Age Group Competitions. These are open to ASA registered swimmers of clubs affiliated to that county. Entry to these may, or may not, have qualifying times. A county may stage a Time Trial or an open competition, providing it conforms to ASA law on Open Competitions.

● ASA District Championships and Age Group Competitions, open to clubs affiliated to a particular district. The qualifying times for entry will be harder than those generally found in county events. Some ASA districts organise their championships to allow entries to be accepted from ASA registered swimmers who may be seeking to achieve a national qualifying time but who are from outside the district.

● A Designated Meet. This may be an area event, or time trial, organised by a county, club, or an association affiliated to a district. The organising body must apply for approval to the Honorary Secretary of the ASA district in which the meet is to be held. A fee will be levied and the district will apply conditions as to how the event is to be organised.

● The National Championships of the ASA, the qualifying times of which are set at a level at which only the stronger, fitter, and more able competitor will achieve. Competitors at this level usually belong to a club that has a great deal of water time. The broad base for producing the elite athlete requires a facility that is available for up to 20 hours or more per week, and a "squad" system with a well qualified, full time, (usually a professional) coach with dedicated part-time professional and/or amateur support to back him up. Some of these will be either wholly or partly sponsored schemes, supported by Local Authorities or local business firms. Others may be well organised clubs who have a good working relationship with their local pool management. The vast majority of the elite athletes who compete in the Grand Prix Meets, British, European and World Cup Finals, Olympics, World and European Championships come from well organised bases.

The Elite Club

The limitations of "The Elite Club" are controlled by several factors:

● a very good working relationship with the authority controlling the pool facility;

● suitable pools for training. Ideally, this means the main pool 25 or 50 metres long for the top squad, available for an appropriate time each week spread over five or six days for the distances over which all major events are swum, but with satellite pools for squads of various levels of ability;

● pools being available at a suitable time of day, especially the evening sessions that need to fit in with travel, work, college, school, homework, etc., often this will also mean early morning training, so ease of access is essential;

- if the pool time is shared with the public, there must be exclusive use of certain lanes at established times known to the public as well as the trainees;
- the pool should have lane ropes in place at times when training, with starting blocks and Backstroke turning flags to be available when required;
- some exclusive use of the whole facility at certain times during the week and weekend;
- the availability of highly qualified teachers/coaches, professional or amateur, with a good administration team to co-ordinate the financial and technical requirements;
- the need to have a well written **legal** agreement between the club and the pool authority. This is best done professionally.

Outside the running and organisation of the training scheme there will be an enormous amount of work involved in running the remainder of the club. Expertise will be needed in running galas, budgeting and planning for competitions involving travel and accommodation, some of which might be overseas.

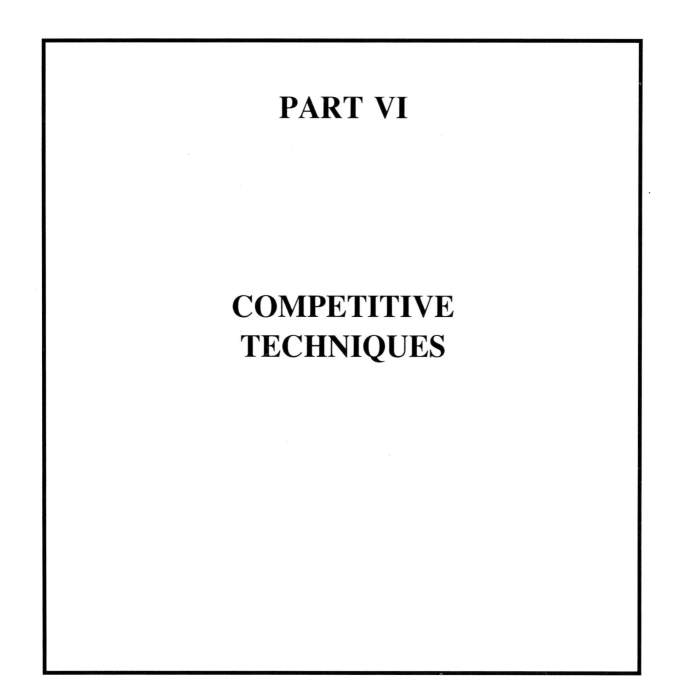

PART VI

COMPETITIVE TECHNIQUES

Introduction to Part VI

Level 1 in the series dealt with the basic strokes. Clearly, for those who wish to go on in the sport, there are additional competition techniques to be covered, e.g., starting, turning, etc. Furthermore, as more involvement in competition develops, the techniques for Individual Medley (IM) and Team Medley events usually become important. Part VI takes up these aspects of the competitive programme. In addition, Part VI returns to the issue of analysis and its related techniques. It was introduced in *Level 1* of the series, but it is important to emphasize that the need for sound analytical techniques, if improvement is to be continued, never goes away.

Chapter 14

Starts, Turns and Finishes

Lynn Hogarth

Introduction

Starts and finishes are part of every competitive swimming race. Whilst turns also form a part of many competitive races, they are also necessary when carrying out any kind of swimming activity which involves one or more laps of the pool, e.g., lane swimming. Effective starting and turning places the swimmer's body in the correct position to commence a swimming stroke. Furthermore, the swimmer's initial speed from the block/starting platform or wall is greater than that reached when actually swimming, consequently the swimmer is in the fortunate position of decreasing momentum before swimming rather than trying to increase it whilst swimming.

Effective starting, turning and finishing can be measured in two different ways:
- technically efficiency;
- speed efficiency.

Usually the speed efficient swimmer is also technically efficient, although the reverse is not always true.

It is not always necessary for the swimmer to have both technical and speed efficiency, e.g., a young swimmer in a swimming lesson needs to master a turn which is technically efficient, but speed at this stage is not a priority. The needs and the aims of the individual, therefore, must be considered when teaching/ coaching a start, turn or finish.

Competitively, it is essential that a swimmer is efficient in both areas. All too often a race is lost due to poor starting, turning or finishing. An improved start can reduce race time by at least 0.1 seconds. Improved turns can reduce race time by at least 0.2 seconds per length and an improved finish can reduce race time by at least 0.1 seconds. Whilst such improvements would be significant in 100m races, their impact on the longer distances would be even more so. Much time is spent on swimming training each week with often small rewards. Just one hour's practice per week on starts, turns and finishes could reduce a 100m time by 0.8 seconds even for an elite competitor. This would be significant for a top class swimmer.

ASA laws

Starts, turns and finishes within a swimming race must be performed in accordance with the current ASA laws. Teachers/coaches, or those intending to use the turns in a race situation, should ensure that they are familiar with current laws (see Part VII, Additional Information).

Safety
Teachers/coaches should pay particular attention to the safety implications for head first entries (See Chapters 10 and 15).

Mechanics of start and turns

Balance

Everybody has a centre of gravity (C of G) which is located roughly around the abdominal area. When the centre of gravity remains within that area balance is maintained. Once the centre of gravity moves outside that area the body overbalances. This principle explains the importance of a good stance when executing a start.

The stance

A swimmer should strive for a stance:

- which maintains balance and a comfortable position. Swimmers must be still before the starting signal can be given. An off-balance position could result in a false start and, possibly, disqualification;
- which enables the swimmer to get off the block as quickly as possible after the starting signal, i.e., a position where the centre of gravity is just behind front edge of the block. (See Fig. 14.1)

Take off/Push off velocity

This is the measurement of a swimmer's speed off the block or wall. It is affected by three main factors:

- the amount of force applied to the block or wall by the swimmer's leg thrust;
- the swimmer's reaction time from hearing the starting signal;
- the speed of a swimmer's approach to the wall and rotation during a turn.

Figure 14.1 Relationship of Centre of Gravity with front edge of starting platform – Grab start stance

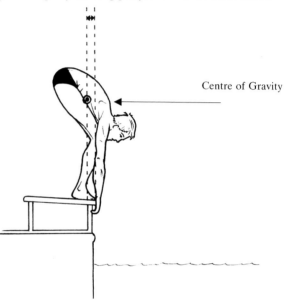

Centre of Gravity

Rotation

During a dive trajectory the body rotates in order to enter the water head first. All turns use a form of rotation to get into and out of the wall. Rotation in starts and turns can be executed in two ways:

- Piked – bending at the hips whilst the rest of the body remains straight (See Fig. 14.2(a));
- Tucked – the body bends at the hips with the knees being drawn up to the chest bringing the feet close to the buttocks (See Fig. 14.2(b)).

Figure 14.2(a) Rotation (piked) during flight

Figure 14.2(b) Rotation (tucked) during flight

Whilst the most commonly used rotation in starts is in the piked position, both types of rotation can often be seen in turns.

Transfer of Momentum

The momentum gained from the take off thrust in the dive can be utilised to aid the speed at which the body travels in water. As the swimmer enters the water the body travels downwards at speed. This speed is transferred into forwards motion by arching the back and lifting the head and hands. Similarly, the speed of a swimmer's approach and rotation at the turn will give momentum which can be transferred into the push off and transition.

Forward starts

Butterfly, Breaststroke and Freestyle (for the purposes of this chapter, Front Crawl) races normally start with a dive from a starting block or poolside. The most commonly used starts are:

- Grab Start;
- Track Start;
- Swing Start.

Each of the above is normally broken down into:

- **Stance** – the position on the block;
- **Take Off** – the departure from the block. The angle at take off will affect the height of flight and, consequently, the depth of entry. Modern diving technique advocates a high angle of take off to allow a better transfer of momentum from downwards to forwards;
- **Flight** – the movements which are observed whilst the swimmer is in the air;
- **Entry** – the path the body follows into the water;
- **Transition to Stroke** – how a swimmer changes from streamlining during entry into the stroke itself.

The Grab Start

Stance (See Fig. 14.1)

- the toes should grip the front edge of the starting block or poolside by curling the toes around the edge;
- the feet should be approximately shoulder width apart in a position which the swimmer finds stable and comfortable;
- the knees should be flexed to approximately 30-40 degrees. The swimmer's back should be curved with the head down and looking at the water just beyond the starting block. These three points of technique ensure that the centre of gravity is correctly positioned;
- the hands should grip the block either inside or outside the swimmer's feet. The position of the hands is usually the choice of the swimmer.

Take Off (See Fig. 14.3)

- the swimmer should pull on the block to overbalance the body. This pulling action causes the elbows and knees to flex, with the increased flexion of the knees allowing more force to be applied to the block during departure;
- the feet and legs drive the body outwards and upwards;
- the arms extend upwards and forwards with the finger tips aiming at the point of entry. The finger tips should continue to point in this direction throughout flight;

- as the swimmer begins the initial fall or overbalancing the head should lift and the eyes look up;
- the head should drop and the eyes look at the water just prior to the completion of the leg drive.

For details of **Flight, Entry** and **Transition to stroke** see pages 146-147.

Figure 14.3 Grab start – take off

The Track Start

Figure 14.4 Track start – stance

Stance (See Fig. 14.4)

This position is so named because it resembles that of an athlete on the track:

- the swimmer should place one foot on the front edge of the block with toes curled round the edge and the other foot approximately 20-25cms behind. Both legs should be flexed;
- the centre of gravity should be slightly further back than in the Grab Start due to the position of the feet. The swimmer's weight should be over the front foot;
- the hands should hold the front of the block, approximately shoulder width apart;
- the head should be down with the eyes looking at the water just beyond the edge of the starting block.

Take off (see Fig. 14.5)

- the swimmer should pull upwards on the starting block so as to bring the centre of gravity beyond the front of it;

Figure 14.5 Track start – take off

- the elbows should flex and knee flexion should be increased as the swimmer pulls on the block. This increased knee flexion will allow more force to be applied to the block;
- the drive upwards and outwards should come mainly from the front foot;
- the arms should extend upwards and forwards, and the finger tips aim at the entry point throughout the take off and flight;
- when the swimmer pulls downwards on the block to initiate the fall or overbalancing the head lifts and the eyes look upwards;
- the head should drop and the eyes look at the water just prior to the completion of the leg drive;
- with the completion of the leg drive the trailing leg should be lifted towards the leading leg.

For details of **Flight, Entry** and **Transition to stroke** see page 146-147.

The Swing Start

Prior to the introduction of the Grab Start the Swing Start was normally used. However, the simpler mechanics of the Grab Start has made it a firm favourite. The Swing Start has still remained in use, however, primarily for relay takeovers since, unlike a normal race start, swimmers are permitted to move providing their feet are still on the block when the incoming swimmer touches. The Swing Start allows the swimmer to take advantage of the arm swing to improve both take off velocity and split second timing of the takeover.

Stance (See Fig. 14.6)

- the swimmer's feet should be placed on the edge of the block approximately shoulder width apart with the toes curled over the edge;
- the knees should be slightly flexed, as in the Grab Start;
- the body should bend at the waist so that the angle between the swimmer's upper leg and body is approximately 80 degrees;
- the head should be tucked between the arms, with the eyes looking at the water just in front of the starting block;
- the fingertips point at the water approximately 60cms in front of the block.

Figure 14.6 Swing start – stance and commencement of arm swing

145

Figure 14.7 Swing start – take off and continuation of arm swing

Take Off (See Fig. 14.7)

- the arms circle in a long arc from their starting point upwards, then backwards;
- the arms should remain straight, with the head lifted;
- as the arms circle, the legs should flex until the knees are bent to approximately 90 degrees;
- the circular movement of the arms should be continued round passed the hips, finishing with the hands pointing to the water;
- as the arms complete the circular movement the legs should thrust upwards and outwards against the block, with the head dropping as the legs extend.

For details of **Flight, Entry** and **Transition to stroke** see below.

All Dive Starts

Whilst the stance and take off in each of the above dives differs considerably, the flight and entry are very similar.

Flight – all three dives (See Fig. 14.8(a) and (b))

The flight forms an arc through the air. Once a swimmer has completed the take off the body will be moving in an upwards and outwards direction with the hands pointing at the water.

- as the swimmer reaches the peak of the arc the body should then rotate in either a piked or tucked position, with the direction of the flight being downwards and forwards;
- the pike is achieved by lowering the head and lifting the hips. The hands should be closer to the water than the feet.

Figure 14.8(a) All dive starts – commencement of flight

Figure 14.8(b) All dive starts – example of piked position prior to entry

Entry (See Fig. 14.9(a) and (b))

The entry in to the water should be achieved with as little turbulence as possible in order to minimise drag and ensure that the momentum gained during take off and flight is not wasted;

- the hands should enter the water first, with the remainder of the body following through the same point of entry;
- as the hips enter the water the swimmer's back should arch and the hand lift towards the surface. This movement will ensure the transfer of momentum from downwards to forwards. The point at which the swimmer arches the back is very important since, if it occurs too early, the swimmer's feet will hit the water behind the point at which the hands entered, whereas, if it occurs too late the swimmer will be too deep. The amount of back arch and hand lift will also be dependent upon which stroke is being swum and, consequently, which transition is being used.

Figure 14.9(a) Entry – early phase   *Figure 14.9(b) Entry – final phase.*

Transition to Stroke

After entry the swimmer should take up a streamlined position which will allow the body to move through the water utilizing the momentum gained earlier in the start. The swimmer's speed at this point will probably be greater than race pace, and a successful transition will rely on the swimmer changing from dive to stroke at precisely the right moment, i.e., when dive speed reaches swimming speed;

Butterfly – from the streamlined position the swimmer should begin to kick in a dolphin action to the surface. As the swimmer approaches the surface the hands and arms should move through the propulsive keyhole phase of the arm action. This will assist the swimmer in reaching the surface just as the arms are ready to leave the water;

Breaststroke – the swimmer should be deeper in the water than on any other stroke to allow for the underwater arm and leg actions which are permitted under ASA law. As the swimmer reaches race speed the arms should pull in a keyhole pattern down towards the hips. Once this action is complete the legs should kick with the body taking up a streamlined position ready to surface. As the body surfaces the hands may begin the outsweep of the first arm action of the stroke;

Front Crawl – this is the shortest of all transitions because the Front Crawl is the fastest competitive stroke and, therefore, swimming speed is reached very quickly. From the streamlined position the swimmer should begin to kick the legs in either a Front Crawl or Butterfly action. As the swimmer nears the surface the propulsive phase of the arm action will begin as the propelling arm itself reaches the surface of the water.

Back Crawl Start

Although the Back Crawl start can still be defined as a dive, the start, or stance, position is in the water and, therefore, restricts the height a swimmer is able to gain during flight.

Figure 14.10 Back Crawl start – stance

Stance (See Fig. 14.10)
- the feet should be placed on the wall with the toes below the surface. The feet can either be placed at the same level or slightly staggered, i.e., one higher than the other;
- the knees should be bent to an angle of approximately 70 degrees, with the back rounded, and the head tucked forward on to the chest;
- the hands should hold the starting block in a position which allows the swimmer to keep the knees bent and the back rounded. The elbows should be slightly bent.

Take Off (See Fig. 14.11)
- at the starting signal the elbows should flex to pull the swimmer closer to the starting block. This action will increase the bend at the knees and bring the buttocks closer to the heels. At this point most of the body will be out of the water;
- the hands should release their hold on the block and the head should be forced backwards and slightly upwards;
- the push from the feet should be upwards and outwards from the wall;
- the back should be arched and the arms thrown over the water;

Figure 14.11 Back Crawl start – commencement of take off

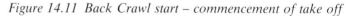

- the throw of the arms should be either in a straight arc from the starting block to the point of entry, or in a semi-circular swing around the side of the body keeping hands and arms close to the water surface;
- the legs should vigorously extend so that when the swimmer leaves the wall the legs and ankles will be fully extended.

Flight (See Fig. 14.12(a) and (b))
As in a forward dive the body travels over the water in an arc:
- after the take off the swimmer will be travelling in an upwards and outwards direction with the whole body streamlined;
- the direction of travel will be changed as the swimmer arches the back and extends the neck so that the other end of the pool can be seen. Ideally, the whole of the swimmer should be out of the water at this point.

Figure 14.12(a) Back Crawl start – flight, early phase

Figure 14.12(b) Back Crawl start – flight, later phase

Entry (See Fig. 14.13)

- the entry should be made with the hands first. The hands will be together and the head between the arms;
- as the hands enter, the hips should be lifted;
- as the hips enter the feet should be lifted;
- on entry the back should be straightened and the fingers pointed to the surface in order to transfer momentum into a forwards direction.

Figure 14.13 Back Crawl start – entry point

Transition to stroke

- from the streamlined position the swimmer should begin to kick using either a Back Crawl leg or dolphin action (note the requirements of the stroke law);
- as the swimmer nears the surface the propulsive phase of the arm action should begin;
- the transition will be completed as the swimmer breaks the surface with the propelling arm ready to begin recovery.

Turns

The recognised competitive turns to be described are, at present, the fastest methods of approaching and leaving the wall within the ASA laws. All teachers/coaches must remember that these turns are not the only correct methods of turning. There are many other ways, perhaps much simpler, than those described, e.g., the touch turn on Front Crawl, but they are certainly not as efficient.

When describing a turn it is broken down into four sections:

- Approach;
- Touch/Turn;
- Push Off;
- Transition to stroke.

The transition to stroke has already been explained in detail under the heading of starts.

Butterfly/Breaststroke turn (See Fig. 14.14)

Approach

- the swimmer should approach the wall at normal swimming speed, making adjustment to stroke length in order to make the touch with arms almost at full stretch;
- the shoulders should remain level during the approach.

Touch/Turn

- the touch should be made with both hands simultaneously. The hands need to fix onto the wall firmly and clearly;
- as the touch is made the knees should bend and the hips should continue to move towards the wall utilizing the forward momentum gained during swimming. This should cause the elbows to bend;
- as soon as the touch has been made the swimmer should release one hand from the wall and pull the elbow backwards. The head should turn to the same side;
- the knees and feet should be drawn up under the body and move towards the wall; and the other hand should be released from the wall and thrown over the water, bending across the face or over the head;
- during the turning action the swimmer should not turn to face the course. It should be a pivoting action.

Push Off

- the feet should be planted firmly on the wall with the toes pointing sideways and downwards;
- the body should drop below the water surface and the swimmer's hands should meet in an extended position beyond the head;
- the swimmer should extend the legs into a streamlined position by thrusting powerfully against the wall;
- the body should leave the wall with the swimmer on the breast, ready to begin the transition to stroke.

Figure 14.14 Butterfly/Breaststroke sequence

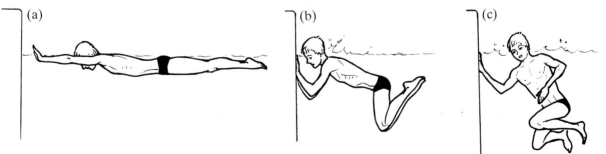

150

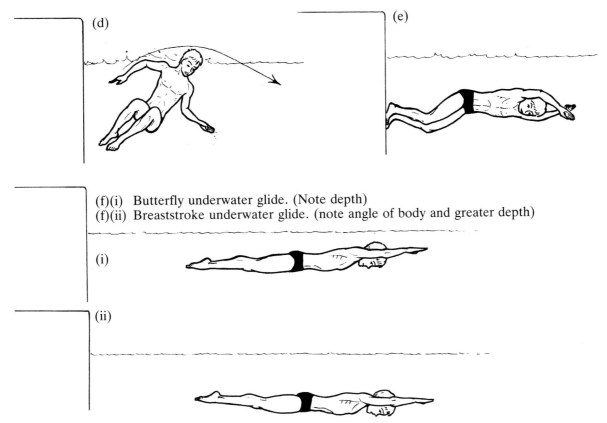

(d)

(e)

(f)(i) Butterfly underwater glide. (Note depth)
(f)(ii) Breaststroke underwater glide. (note angle of body and greater depth)

(i)

(ii)

Front Crawl Turn (usually known as *"The Tumble")* (See Fig. 14.15 on page 152)

Approach
- the swimmer should approach the wall at normal swimming speed;
- as the last over water arm recovery is made prior to turning, the head should drop and the chin rest on the chest.

Turn/Touch
- as the swimmer completes the approach the head should be forced down and the body piked at the hips. This both initiates rotation in the vertical plane and allows forward momentum to be continued;
- the leading arm should pull through to the hip whilst, to assist the speed of rotation, the body should tuck;
- both hands, now alongside the swimmer's body, should press palms downwards, to further assist in the rotation;
- both feet should be planted firmly on the wall for an immediate push off.

Push Off
- the feet should be planted firmly on the wall with the knees bent to an angle of approximately 90 degrees;

151

- the hands and arms should be extended into a streamlined position beyond the head (at this point the swimmer will be virtually on the back);
- the swimmer should extend the legs into a streamlined position by thrusting powerfully against the wall;
- the turn onto the front should occur during the push off phase;
- the swimmer should now be in a streamlined position and ready to begin the transition to the stroke.

NB Twisting during the vertical movement rotation should be avoided to eliminate the possibility of injury to the back.

Figure 14.15 Front Crawl turn (Tumble) sequence

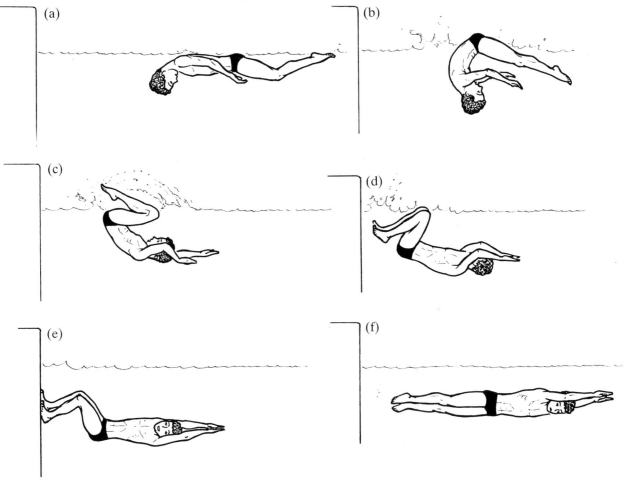

(g)

Backstroke Turn (See Fig. 14.16)

The Backstroke (for the purposes of this chapter, Back Crawl) turning laws now allow a greater variety of legal turning techniques. The turns seen previously, such as the Spin Turn and the Tumble Turn are now rarely used. The turn described in detail is currently the most efficient permitted under the laws:

Approach
- the swimmer should approach the wall on the back. On the last full stroke the swimmer should cross the recovering arm over the body and enter it in line with the opposite shoulder;
- as the arm crosses over the body the swimmer should roll on to the front;
- the other arm should remain at the swimmer's side.

Turn/Touch
- from the position on the front the swimmer should drop the head and rest the chin on the chest;
- the body should pike at the waist and begin a front somersault, assisted by the leading hand. The somersault may be executed with the legs in either a piked or tucked position.

Push Off
- the feet should be planted firmly on the wall with the toes pointing upwards and knees bent to an angle of approximately 90 degrees;
- the leading arm should be extended in front of the head and the other arm should move from the side of the body to meet it;
- the swimmer should extend the legs into a streamlined position by thrusting powerfully against the wall;
- the body should leave the wall with the swimmer in a fully extended, streamlined position ready to begin the transition. Dolphin kicks may be used in this phase, but this depends on the swimmer's kicking ability.

Figure 14.16 Back Crawl turn sequence

(a)

Figure 14.16 continued

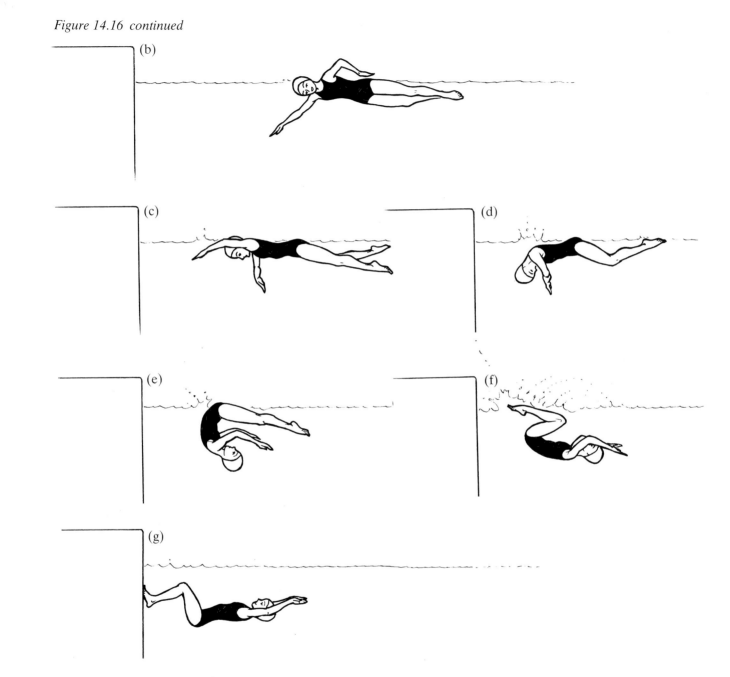

(b)

(c)

(d)

(e)

(f)

(g)

(h)

Finishes

Clearly, there is only one finish in every individual event. In a close race this can mean the difference between winning and losing. Many swimmers have lost races by gliding into the wall but, equally, many swimmers have also lost races by taking too many strokes. It follows, therefore, that finishing techniques need to be practised to ensure that each swimmer knows how to make minor adjustments to stroke length and speed in order to execute the perfect finish. Crowded training lanes do not encourage good finishing and, if this skill is to be practised effectively, swimmers must be placed in a race type situation during training.

Although there is only one finish in an individual race there are four finishes in a team relay. The outgoing swimmer has a right to expect the incoming swimmer to finish **positively.** Any doubts or hesitation could, at best, result in poor placings or times and, at worst, in a team disqualification.

Key points which should be considered when teaching/coaching race finishes:

- always finish on a full stroke;
- maintain the kick until the touch is made;
- finish at speed;
- make a determined commitment to finish strongly at all costs.

Monitoring starts and turns

If improvement is to be measured in starts and turns it is necessary for monitoring to be carried out on a regular basis and, ideally, under race conditions. The ways in which start and turn efficiency can be measured have been mentioned earlier in this chapter and in chapter 5.

Chapter 15

Relay Techniques

Lynn Hogarth

Introduction

Relay events have been an integral part of swimming for many years, yet little information can be found with regard to good practice and the skills of teaching/coaching the basic principles involved. Most teachers/coaches, however, will have used relay races within their sessions to stimulate swimmers to test the skills they have acquired, be it in a beginners' class or at elite level.

The competitive events

There are two recognised relay events, the Freestyle Relay and the Medley Relay. These are swum throughout the spectrum of competitive swimming, although the distances involved may vary. At major international competition it is quite common to see a 4 × 200m Freestyle Relay, whereas at club level any distance from 4 × 100m to 4 × 25m is the norm. It is also common to see relay events of a different format to the above within inter-club competition, e.g., Breaststroke relays. In fact, it is not unusual to see whole galas devoted to relay races, using the innumerable combinations of strokes and distances.

Water depth and safety

Any head first entry is potentially hazardous. This is probably more applicable to relay takeovers than in the individual events. The departing swimmer has a great deal of information to process whilst waiting to enter the water, consequently the issue of water depth becomes one of several, and the safety element may, therefore, be of less importance in the swimmers' mind than it might be in individual events. Teachers/coaches are strongly urged to remain vigilant on matters concerning potential hazards, particularly when less experienced swimmers are involved. The ASA constantly reviews the safety implications of head first entries and the attention of teachers/coaches is particularly drawn to Chapter 10. In addition, teachers/coaches should try to make themselves aware of any further publications or rulings which may appear on the subject (see Part VII, Additional Information).

Freestyle Relay

As the title indicates, swimmers taking part in this event are permitted to use any swimming stroke. Swimmers will normally use Front Crawl because it is the fastest of the swimming strokes. All of the "legs" in a Freestyle Relay begin with a dive start, although starting in the water is permitted by the laws but, usually, only the less experienced swimmers do this, often for reasons of water depth and safety. Each "leg" is completed when the swimmer touches the finishing end of the pool. There are no rules governing the way in which the touch is made.

Medley Relay

This race is a combination of strokes and is swum in the order, Backstroke, Breaststroke, Butterfly and Freestyle. ASA law stipulates that the Freestyle "leg" in a Medley relay can be any stroke other than the three strokes previously swum. This "leg", therefore, is normally swum on Front Crawl.

The first "leg" (Backstroke) in a Medley Relay begins with the swimmer in the water. All the laws relating to a normal Backstroke start apply. The other "legs" begin with a dive start or, perhaps, with the swimmer in the water. Each "leg" is completed when the swimmer touches the finishing end. Both the start and finish of each "leg" of a Medley Relay must comply with the appropriate ASA stroke laws (see Part VII, Additional Information).

The Relay Takeover

Relay races can be won or lost on the efficiency of the takeovers, so it is important for all teachers/coaches to understand the ASA laws relating to takeovers and to ensure that swimmers have ample opportunity to practise these skills correctly.

The ASA law states that the outgoing swimmer should remain in contact with the end of the pool or starting block until the incoming swimmer touches. It should be noted, however, that this does not mean that the swimmer must remain still. All swimmers in a relay race, other than the first "leg", are permitted to move as the incoming swimmer approaches the wall. A good takeover can be seen when the swimmer's feet are ready to leave the wall/block the moment the touch is made. It is difficult for the human eye to judge the perfect takeover, and in order to achieve a good takeover the incoming swimmer and outgoing swimmer must be aware of their roles.

Incoming swimmer

The finish of the incoming swimmer's "leg" is of the upmost importance because the outgoing swimmer cannot stop the momentum once the commitment to dive has been made:

- **speed of approach** – at approximately 5 metres from finish the swimmer should make a commitment to finish **hard** and **accurately;**
- **touch** – the touch must be positive and without hesitation or glide;
- **after touch** – the swimmer should bring the knees into the chest to leave clear water for the outgoing swimmer's dive.

Outgoing swimmer

It is advantageous to use a swing start (See Chapter 14) because this allows momentum to be gathered before the outgoing swimmer leaves the wall/block. It also permits adjustments in balance to allow for any mistake by the incoming swimmer. Any preparatory movement of the body prior to the incoming swimmer touching will improve the overall speed of the team swim. The teaching/coaching of the outgoing swimmer in a relay event will often mean the introduction of a new diving technique in addition to the timing involved in the takeover. The teaching/coaching of the outgoing swimmer should emphasize:

- familiarity with the swing start;
- judgement of pace of the incoming swimmer;
- the commencement of the arm swing prior to the touch;
- commitment to accurately completing the dive once the movement has commenced.

If the outgoing swimmers are to execute a good takeover they **must have confidence** in the finishing commitment of the incoming swimmer.

Timing of relay events

When swimmers compete in relay races it is normal for the teacher/coach to time each one individually. These times can provide important information regarding both future team selection and the order in which swimmers race in the team. The timing of the first "leg" in a team race is identical to that of an individual event. A swimmer, therefore, is able to break an individual record when swimming in a team event providing it occurs during the first "leg". For the reasons already described, all the times for the other swimmers reflect a moving start and, therefore, will be faster than the start of an individual event.

Selecting the team

Swimmers' performances in relay and individual events are often quite different. It is essential, therefore, that teachers/coaches assess swimmers during relay race work. A comparison of swimmer's individual and relay times can, of course, assist in the selection of the best team.

In a Freestyle Relay the order in which swimmers compete is also very important. Some swimmers will compete better on the first "leg", whilst others like to "bring the race home". Teachers/coaches should assess swimmers takeover techniques carefully when deciding the order of swimming in Freestyle Relays.

Practices for relay events

There are many different ways of introducing relay techniques to all levels of swimmers. At this stage it is important to highlight that good practice and sportsmanship are essential areas of concern at all levels of learning.

Non-swimmers' relays – it is best to base these relays around activities which allow the non-swimmers to stand, walk or run in shallow water. This will make the task achievable for all the pupils in the class:

- short distance running races;
- hopping or jumping races;
- blowing an object across the pool races;
- passing a float or other object (as in passing a baton in a running relay).

All these activities are simple to organise and can be achieved with or without artificial aids. They are an excellent method of distracting the pupils' attention away from possible fears of the water – indeed, they are fun!

Weak swimmers' relays
- any of the races for non-swimmers;
- kicking races with floats. Vary the type of action used.

Improvers' relays – these races should still be swum over short distances, i.e., one width per swimmer:

- kicking races with or without floats. Vary leg action used;
- full stroke races starting in the water;
- races with a dive start;
- introduction to the competitive events.

Early competitive swimmers – it is important at this level to ensure that swimmers understand the formal procedures and laws relating to the relay events:

- takeover practices. These allow swimmers to improve their incoming and outgoing takeover techniques without the pressure of racing. It is also an activity which involves continuous practice for many pupils at the same time, and makes good use of water space;
- "Handicap" relay races. These give the swimmers a chance to practise under pressure and with good handicapping, i.e., delayed starts based on previous times, providing close, exciting races.

Experienced competitive swimmers – an important factor for these swimmers is to appreciate that split-second timing can make the difference between winning, losing or being disqualified:

- takeover practices at race speed. The organisation of this practice should be as for early competitive swimmers;
- race situation relays. This gives experienced swimmers the opportunity to practice under pressure, as in a race;
- competition team practice. A team performance is always enhanced if the swimmers involved have had an opportunity to practice **as a team.**

Summary

Teachers/coaches and swimmers should be constantly aware that the various relay skills need as much, perhaps even more, serious practice as that given to the individual events.

- relay events are an important aspect of team competition;
- in a team competition the points for relay events are **at least** the same as those given to individual events but, often, they can be **double** the value.

Chapter 16

The Individual Medley

Ian Oliver

Introduction

Though not classified as a stroke in its own right, the Individual Medley (usually known as the "IM") is a recognised competition event. It is a combination of the four competition strokes and is swum in the order of Butterfly, Backstroke, Breaststroke and Freestyle. Freestyle may not be one of the other three strokes. The IM is the latest individual event to be added to the Olympic programme and appeared for the first time in 1964 at the Tokyo Olympics, when Richard Roth won the Men's 400 metres in 4 mins 45.4 secs, and Donna De Varona won the women's event in 5 mins 18.7 secs. The 200 metres IM was introduced at the 1968 Olympic Games.

Its late appearance on the Olympic scene may be the reason why so little has been written about it, though its history goes back into the 1920's. At that time it was, of course, a three stroke event swum only in the USA National Championships. It became a four stroke event after the separation of Breaststroke and Butterfly into individual events in 1953, although it was not included in the English Championships until 1963. There are several particular values over and above the other individual events/strokes:

- it is acknowledged as an all round skill performed by the complete swimmer, and is regarded by many as the doyen of strokes;
- for many swimmers with high all round ability, but with no specific strength to make them leaders in an individual event, it offers an opportunity to be a winner;
- its changes in tempo and pace often result in sudden exciting fluctuations in race positions, and so it is popular with both spectators and swimmers;
- it is thought to be an excellent training device for all round development. Indeed, it was used in this way long before it became a recognised race event in its own right. The importance of the training principle of **variety** has made the IM an even more purposeful method of training.

It is true to say that the IM is now an essential part of every training programme. It must be stressed, too, that, with its unique qualities of multiple skill and changes of pace and tempo, it is also an essential for the total development of the age group swimmer. The ability to swim all strokes, to switch from one tempo and pace to another and to achieve success in doing so, will play a major part in establishing the base for a strong swimming career. Furthermore, it contributes to children gaining more widely based experiences.

It is often the case that, in the search for quick success, less experienced coaches will set up narrowly focused programmes with young swimmers performing on one stroke only. This can only contribute to eventual failure, early retirement and even possible injury of the overuse type. Swimming various types of medley will help in avoiding these pitfalls. It is clear, too, that, in terms of conditioning, IM can make an enormous contribution to complete all round physiological development. Its importance in this respect also extends into warm-up and swim-down when attention to the total muscular structure is vital.

Individual Medley competition

Since the individual medley is a combination event concerning all four strokes swum in a certain order, it is important that swimmers and teachers/coaches are aware of the current laws of each stroke and **how they are applied in this event.** The laws of turning, particularly, differ at the change over to another stroke. These differences must be practised in training if disqualification is to be avoided. Ignorance of the laws is no excuse, and teachers/coaches and swimmers must keep abreast of current laws. The swimming strokes are detailed in *"Teaching and Coaching – Level 1",* but there are some points of special importance to this event.

Butterfly

This stroke is the platform from which the whole race is launched. It must be swum competently, maintaining sound technique and with no excessive strain which will detract from the quality of the next stroke. Backstroke must not be a rest from the Butterfly "leg" of the race. For the novice or less experienced swimmer Butterfly is a part of the race to get out of the way, rather than being seen as the launch pad. Butterfly is usually the last stroke learned, and probably the least efficient, therefore, it is important to maintain an efficient breathing pattern. Regular and complete air intake is essential to avoid excessive early fatigue build up in the event, with a subsequent deterioration in the other strokes. This can lead to an incorrect coach assessment of strokes with the coach seeking to improve the later strokes when, in reality, the problem has been created earlier during the Butterfly.

In the early stages of IM swimming, or for swimmers whose Butterfly is weak, it may be necessary in training to modify this first "leg" by swimming Butterfly to the point of stroke deterioration, then finishing the distance with a less strenuous Butterfly drill. The aim will then be to steadily increase the distance of the weak stroke until the necessary quality is reached. Swimmers should normally only be permitted to enter the IM event when their Butterfly is up to standard. Disqualification, disappointment and disillusion with the event can then be avoided.

Backstroke

Again, the emphasis is on maintaining a good technique and skilfully transferring from the simultaneous stroke into the different rhythm and tempo of the alternating action. As mentioned earlier, the novice will often seek to rest after the exertion of the Butterfly. Obviously, the quality of the Butterfly has to be addressed, but so, too, does the mental approach.

Swimmers lacking flexibility, often they are Breaststroke orientated, frequently find Backstroke a weakness, and this is often recognised by an inefficient kick. Backstroke, (for the purposes of this chapter the stroke will be referred to as Back Crawl) because of the lateral nature of the pull, requires a strong kick to maintain body position. Swimmers can compensate for lack of shoulder flexibility, but not for weak kicking. Plenty of kicking practice is a must. It has often been observed that top IM swimmers have a first class Back Crawl. It is essential that, during the first few strokes, the swimmer concentrates on stroke quality, and gradually builds up the effort as the "leg" proceeds.

Breaststroke

This is the slowest of the individual strokes and, therefore, the slowest part of the IM. It does not necessarily follow that the Breaststroke specialist will excel in this phase of the medley; the ability to change tempo seems to play a big part in this section. If this ability is high, then the Breaststroke swimmer will often be seen surging through the field. In the early days of the event Breaststroke was said to be **the** important factor. Certainly the performances of Anita Lonsborough in the sixties, and of David Wilkie, World Record holder in 1974, tended to reinforce this thinking. It is true that the greatest percentage of race time is spent on the Breaststroke "leg" and, therefore, any differences in time are greater and any stroke defect more apparent. High quality Breaststroke is essential, though not at the expense of the other strokes.

The technique of the Breaststroke required for IM, particularly long-course events, tends to be different from that used in the individual event. The emphasis is even more on the kick and on a longer stroke. The way in which the large leg muscles are used in Breaststroke is different from other strokes and this change is a form of rest which must be utilised to the full.

Freestyle

Freestyle (for the purposes of this chapter the stroke will be referred to as Front Crawl), is the final "leg" of the event and, as with all the other changes, the transfer must be efficient. Although the legs have been used strongly in the Breaststroke section, an immediate strong flutter kick off the wall after the Breaststroke is important, both to transfer the feeling of the change of tempo and to activate the mental processes to focus on the new stroke. Once more, sound technique is the first priority because at this stage the body is tiring and needs to utilise its systems most efficiently. Wasted movement leads to rapid fatigue. It is vital that the swimmer has the fitness to steadily build up to a fast finish.

Race distance and pool length

The distances for this event include:

- 100m – becoming very popular at club level and as a developmental stage. Obviously it is short course only;
- 200m – swum both short course and long course, but is the only IM event available at higher levels for certain age groups. Teachers/Coaches should check current laws carefully;
- 400m – swum both short course and long course for the older age groups. Again teachers/coaches should be aware of current law changes.

100m Individual Medley

This has become very popular since sprint events have been included in the international scene. It is very popular in club competition both in its own right, and as an ideal developmental stage for younger swimmers; though there is one possible drawback, namely, the matter of technique. It has been stressed that technique is of paramount importance in IM. However, in this event it is possible to hide weaknesses and teachers/coaches must be on their guard against this. Nevertheless, it is an excellent event, and is both exciting and great fun.

200m Individual Medley

Technique, or rather the lack of good technique, begins to show in this event, particularly with young developing swimmers. There is less time in the 200 IM short course event to take time to adjust to a new stroke tempo. Swimmers must be able to hit high quality stroke technique immediately after the turns when switching from stroke to stroke. Treating the event aggressively as four sprints is the best approach to the short course medley. Furthermore, it must be stressed that as the race distance for each "leg" decreases, and the pool length reduces, power becomes more important.

The 200m IM swimmer needs to be aggressive and powerful, with well developed muscular co-ordination, to be able to achieve sprint ability and an effective rapid change of tempo.

400m Individual Medley

Again the differences between swimming long course and short course must be considered. In the 400m IM short course, power, though important, plays only an equal role to high aerobic capacity. In the long course event 400m aerobic capacity is the key factor. It would be fair to say that the 400m short course is classed as a middle distance event and the long course more of a distance event.

The good quality stroke technician, too, becomes more obvious in the long course event. This applies particularly to the Breaststroke "leg" of the event.

Figure 16.1 Guidelines for pacing

Stroke	200 metres IM	400 metres IM
Butterfly	50m PBT* + 1 to 1.5 secs	100m PBT* + 2 to 3 secs
Back Crawl	50m PBT* + 3 to 4 secs	100m PBT* + 6 to 7 secs
Breaststroke	50m PBT* + 5 to 6 secs	100m PBT* + 8 to 10 secs
Front Crawl	50m PBT* + 4 secs	100m PBT* + 6 to 7 secs
*PBT = Personal Best Time		

Some teachers/coaches also use a percentage of total race time (TRT) as a guide to correct pace. After analysing many World class swims the following pattern of percentages emerged:

Figure 16.2 Percentage of total race time (TRT)

Stroke	% of Total Race Time	
Butterfly	22.5	
Back Crawl	25.5	
Breaststroke	29.5	
Front Crawl	22.5	

It must be stressed that, whilst the above guidelines have been used successfully by many teachers/coaches, they do not take into account any personal strengths and weaknesses of individual swimmers and, therefore, slavish adherence to these figures might not be appropriate.

Example 1				
Total Race Time (TRT)	Butterfly mins secs	Back Crawl mins secs	Breaststroke mins secs	Front Crawl mins secs
4 min 17.3 secs	1:00.0 23.3% (TRT)	1:04.6 25.0% (TRT)	1:13.3 28.5% (TRT)	0:59.4 23.1% (TRT)

Example 1 would be roughly in line with those shown at Fig. 16.2 on page 163.

Example 2				
Total Race Time (TRT)	Butterfly mins secs	Back Crawl mins secs	Breaststroke mins secs	Front Crawl mins secs
5 min 10.5 secs	1:10.5 22.5% (TRT)	1:21.7 26.3% (TRT)	1:19.3 28.7% (TRT)	1:09.3 22.0% (TRT)

Example 2 represents three split times close to target times. Therefore, this might indicate a Back Crawl weakness. If the Breaststroke and Butterfly split times had been unusually fast it might have indicated some form of compensatory swim.

Example 3				
Total Race Time (TRT)	Butterfly mins secs	Back Crawl mins secs	Breaststroke mins secs	Front Crawl mins secs
4 min 41.4 secs	1:00.4 21.4% (TRT)	1:10.9 25.0% (TRT)	1:25.6 37.5% (TRT)	1:04.5 22.9% (TRT)

Example 3 almost certainly shows a Breaststroke weakness.

Young swimmers often find that Butterfly is their weakest stroke and, as a result, they are very fatigued for the Back Crawl "leg" of the event. In order to minimise this problem it is essential to encourage swimmers to concentrate on the quality and change of rhythm at the start of the Back Crawl "leg".

Training

There are two aspects to training on medley work:
- training **for** the Individual Medley **as a race;**
- using the Individual Medley **as a training device.**

Race Training

In terms of energy costs training, in general, will follow that of normal middle distance training. This, however, covers a wide area and Fig. 16.3 provides an indication of how the balance falls in relation to the Freestyle events:

Balancing the four strokes in training is important. The name **"individual** medley" assumes deeper significance because race training is such an individual matter. There are no strict rules or principles to follow beyond those outlined in the chapter "Methods of Training". Weaknesses have to be ironed out and at the same time strengths developed. Each teacher/coach must produce a balancing act which must vary from one individual to another. In this event individual differences are accentuated, and it is, therefore, a mistake always to apply the same methods to every swimmer.

Figure 16.3 Relationships of Freestyle and IM training

	Sprint	**Middle Distance**	**Distance**
Training IM	50m 100m 100m	200m 400m 200m (SC)* (LC)* 400m (LC)*	800m 1500m 400m (LC)*
*SC = Short course LC = Long course			

In planning the year's programme it is important to begin each major training cycle by working on the strokes individually, and by swimming specific strokes in competition with particular emphasis on any which may be weak. An ability to perform well on each stroke makes IM swimmers useful team members. Teachers/coaches should exploit this for the benefit of both the individual swimmer and the team. Assuming a three cycle year, the single stroke phase should occupy the first third of the first cycle, the first quarter of the second cycle and the first sixth of the final cycle. Gradually, "switch" swimming is introduced to encourage neuromuscular adaptation. "Switch" swimming is covering distances involving the change from stroke to stroke. Initially it is important to vary this type of swimming as much as possible for maximum adaptation. Gradually, "switching" becomes more race specific so that the all-important pacing of various sections can be practised, reinforced and confidence built. Training here also involves "Broken Swims". Competition becomes more orientated toward the major events occurring at the end of the cycle. "Negative split swimming", i.e., practising single strokes with the second half of the repetition distance faster than the first, is important to the IM swimmer. Repetition distances for 200m IM training should be 100m, whilst for the 400m IM the repetition distance should be 200m.

Although starts, turns and finishes are practised during all phases of training, they should receive special attention during the final phase to ensure that essential confidence is developed. Finally, competition in IM should include a study of opponents, their stroke strengths and weaknesses. This applies particularly to the 400m IM. No swimmer should be taken by surprise by a surge on an opponent's strong stroke.

The IM as a training device

Individual Medley should be the basis of all age-group development programmes. No young swimmer should think of specialising in any stroke or event until about 13 or 14 years of age for the girls, and about 15 or 16 years of age for the boys. Before that time age group swimmers should have the broadest possible background and, clearly, Individual Medley is part of that background. It offers:

- multi stroke development;
- important neuromuscular development;
- the opportunity to develop weak areas;
- variety in training;
- an excellent means of introducing and developing overdistance training;
- a method of improving aerobic capacity;
- an essential part of warm-up prior to competition or training.

Individual Medley should not be thought of simply in terms of standard distances. It can be swum on the basis of:

- Distance – this includes both standard and varied distances for the total IM and for each lap;
- Time – this is an excellent group activity controlled by the teacher/coach using a signal, such as a whistle, to change stroke;
- Number of strokes – this is a good way in which to introduce IM, and also to focus attention on the stroke.

Individual Medleys need not be confined to recognised strokes or the pattern of four. Drills, combination strokes, kicking, pulling, using apparatus such as paddles and fins, can all be used to construct interesting medleys. Individual Medley is an ideal basis for the inventive, imaginative teacher/coach to make swimming interesting and enjoyable for all swimmers.

Chapter 17

Skill Observation and Analysis

Lynn Hogarth

Introduction

The basic principles of stroke analysis, together with the recognised procedures and format for handling observation and analysis, were set out in *Level 1* of this series. This chapter will develop the theme, and examine the fundamentals of good techniques with reference to the biomechanics of competitive swimming. The analysis of competitive starts and turns will also be considered.

Observation

The teacher/coach constantly observes technique within a lesson/training session. The observations made in this informal environment will often provide the base from which technique changes can be made. After initial observation, it is then necessary for the teacher/coach to look at technique in greater detail in order to ascertain the effect a change in one aspect of a swimmer's skills (Stroke, starts or turns) may have on other aspects of the stroke, e.g., stroke techniques will vary with intensity and effort. It is important for the teacher/coach to make this initial observation in different training conditions, i.e., Aerobic Endurance (low intensity or extensive training), Anaerobic Endurance (speed endurance), and Speed Training (sprint). In addition, technique should be observed in a competition environment when the swimmer has additional psychological pressures.

Once a swimmer's technique has been viewed in a variety of conditions the teacher/coach can then analyse, in greater detail, with a view to making adjustments or corrections which will result in a more efficient technique and enable the swimmer to vary intensities, speeds, stroke lengths and rates. Teachers/coaches should be aware that changes to technique take a prolonged period of time and require constant observation, cooperation and understanding from the swimmer, especially if the changes initially result in a poor performance.

Stroke Analysis

Structured analysis, following the format in *Level 1* in the series, allows the teacher/coach to break down a stroke into its components and identify the precise area of technique to be adjusted or corrected. It enables the teacher/coach to assess the effect of change on the overall technique, and to apply biomechanical principles to the swimmer's individual style. Furthermore, the teacher/coach will have the opportunity to increase the swimmer's awareness of technique so that s/he learns more about swimming styles and mechanics. This plays an important role in the development of the swimmer. The teacher/coach is the swimmer's eyes and must be able to accurately analyse a technique and provide feedback on how the correct technique should feel. A structured, systematic and consistent method of analysis can provide these useful comparisons.

Analysis methods

Poolside analysis – This is the simplest and most common method of analysis. It has been in use for many years and any teacher/coach can use it. Viewing from the poolside, i.e., above the water, provides a variety of angles which build up a complete picture:

- from the front;
- from the back;
- from both sides;
- from above, e.g., a balcony.

However, the disadvantages of this method are:

- water refraction can make underwater strokes deceptive;
- overwater action is clear, underwater action is blurred;
- lighting problems.

Underwater analysis – Facilities for underwater analysis are scarce. The willing teacher/coach can don a snorkel mask or goggles and view technique from all sides. Underwater analysis allows true observation of the mechnical principles of lift and drag.

Video analysis – Over or underwater video analysis can be of great assistance to the teacher/coach. It provides the opportunity to watch technique repeatedly and, also, to use slow motion, freeze frame and single frame advance. This can pin point the precise areas of technique which need attention. In addition, the swimmer can also view the technique and gain a greater awareness of his/her own style and the adjustments or corrections necessary. Swimmers are usually very surprised when they see their own technique on video and they can learn a great deal from this experience. It is important, however, to carefully control the video viewing time, otherwise the focus of attention deteriorates. Remember, it can always be replayed on a subsequent occasion.

Video analysis also allows for a period of technique change to be recorded and comparisons between old and new style to be made. Furthermore, this method of analysis can be used both under and over the water. Full video recording of competition is also of immense value. Wherever possible such records should include the warm-up and other preliminaries, as well as the actual race techniques. Parents, under careful teacher/coach guidance, can often contribute a great deal to this form of recording.

Analysing the individual

"Text book" strokes are based on scientific evidence which has identified what is believed to be the ideal body position, limb track, breathing technique and pattern. It is impossible for an individual to mirror exactly "The Perfect Stroke". The teacher/coach must take into consideration many individual differences whilst deciding on the best style for each swimmer. Some of the factors to consider are:

- Flexibility
- Buoyancy
- Power/Strength
- Sex
- Age
- Limb size in relation to the body (comparative dimension)
- Fatigue

The teacher/coach must be prepared to alter technique as a young swimmer grows and develops. This can also be seen as a development in the skill of the individual. Such changes in technique, however, will be minimal if the techniques learned in childhood are based on sound biomechanical principles.

Fundamentals of good technique

Good competitive swimmers display certain fundamentals of good technique. It is these fundamentals which differentiate these swimmers from many others. Dr James Counsilman, coach to many world record holders said:

"Good Swimmers rarely violate the basic fundamentals of stroke mechanics, whilst poor swimmers almost always do."

This can be observed quite clearly when watching swimmers of different levels compete.

The teacher/coach must be able to identify these fundamentals and separate them from the less important points. The fundamentals are seen as:

- **Body position** – Flat, streamlined and straight. A good swimmer will not deviate unnecessarily. Any deviation will be eliminated by an effective limb track;
- **Effective Kicking** – In Butterfly, Back Crawl and Front Crawl an effective leg action will give good balance, and so reduce drag. In Breaststroke the leg action needs to give effective propulsion as well as minimalising drag;
- **Effective Sculling** – Propulsion stemming from the lift theory requires effective sculling to produce fast swimming;
- **High Elbow Position** – To use effectively long and short levers a swimmer needs to display a high elbow position at the front end of the stroke;
- **Acceleration** – In order to use the mechanical principles of propulsive lift and propulsive drag theories the hand speed should increase throughout the propulsive phases of the arm actions. Similarly, in Breaststroke the foot speed should increase throughout propulsive phase;
- **Effective recovery movements** – Any recovery which does not create unnecessary drag can be considered effective;
- **Effective Breathing** – Effective breathing will not interfere with the other stroke mechanics, but will allow sufficient time for the gaseous exchanges to take place.

Start and Turn Analysis

In a competition the teacher/coach will be looking for a performance which not only displays the best use of the biomechanical principles relating to each competitive stroke, but also to the competitive starts and turns. Here, again, the teacher/coach needs to be able to observe, analyse and assess before implementing changes. All of the analysis methods already discussed under stroke analysis can be used when analysing starts and turns. It is probably even more important to have access to video analysis in these situations, since there is only a minimal amount of time to observe because both starts and turns occur at speed. To be most effective video playback facilities should include slow motion, reverse and freeze frame options. Furthermore, it should not be forgotten that an essential part of this analysis is teacher/coach discussion with the swimmer during the viewing.

Biomechanical principles of Starts and Turns

The following principles are an outline of the approach to these skills:

- **Balance** – The position of the Centre of Gravity will determine the swimmer's balance and, also, the time it takes to travel over the front of the starting block before the leg drive can commence;

- **Take off velocity** – The speed at which the swimmer leaves the block. This is dependent on the amount of thrust given by the leg drive and the force reaction time;
- **Transfer of Momentum** – Momentum from the thrust can be transferred into forwards speed when the body enters the water. The better the take off velocity, the more effective the transfer of momentum;
- **Rotation** – There are two types of rotation used during starts and turns. When the body is in a tucked position it can be referred to as "closed rotation", and when it is in a piked position, it is said to be "open rotation". The body rotates faster during closed rotation than in open rotation. The precise timing or sequence of these actions is important and should be noted carefully.

Basic competitive start analysis

For analysis purposes a competitive start is broken down into the following components:

- Stance
- Flight
- Transition to stroke
- Take Off
- Entry

As in stroke analysis, each component can be further divided in order to provide the teacher/coach with key areas of technique which may need attention. The teacher/coach should look at all of the areas using the following example in Fig. 17.1:

Figure 17.1 Starts analysis sheet

Name of swimmer .... Age ....

Start to be analysed.. Date ....

STANCE
Position of feet
Position of hips
Position of head
Position of arms
Knee bend
Shape of back

TAKE OFF
Position of head
Position of arms
Angle of take off
Knee bend during take off
Amount of thrust

FLIGHT
Changes in head position
Rotation
Streamlining
Body changes during flight

ENTRY
Position of body on entry
Angle of body at entry

TRANSITION TO STROKE
Streamlining
Transfer of momentum
Speed of body during transition to stroke

Basic Turn Analysis

A turn can also be broken down into its components:

- Approach
- Touch/Turn
- Push Off
- Transition to Stroke

Each component can be further sub-divided to produce a more detailed analysis as in the example in Fig. 17.2:

Figure 17.2   Turns analysis sheet

Name of swimmer .... Age ....

Turn to be analysed .... Date ....

APPROACH
Head position
Speed of approach
Timing of last inhalation
Timing of approach

TOUCH/TURN
Hand position
Rotation
Movement of arms
Movement of legs
Feet plant

PUSH OFF
Knee bend at point of push off
Leg thrust
Position of body during leg thrust
Position of arms

TRANSITION TO STROKE
Streamlining
Speed of body during transition

Only through accurate observation, assessment and analysis can positive changes in technique be made to benefit the swimmer. Analysis may be used at the lowest level to correct basic faults and at the highest level to refine an already sound technique. The ultimate aim should be to improve the swimmer either in terms of speed, or the ease in which the skill is executed. The levels at which the analysis process is used, will differ, **but there are no short cuts to improvement in technique.**

PART VII

ADDITIONAL INFORMATION

FURTHER READING

Alter M.J., (1988) *Science of Stretching,* Human Kinetics

Åstrand P-O. and Rodahl K., (1986) *Textbook of Work Physiology – Physiological bases of exercise,* McGraw-Hill

Colwin C.M., (1992) *Swimming into the 21st Century,* Leisure Press (Human Kinetics [UK] Ltd)

Costill D., Maglischo E. and Richardson A., (1991) *Swimming,* Blackwell Scientific Publications

Counsilman J., (1968) *The Science of Swimming,* Pelham Books

Counsilman J., (1978) *Competitive Swimming Manual for Coaches and Swimmers,* Pelham Books

Cross R., (Edit.) (1987) *The ASA Guide to Better Swimming,* Pan Books

Cross R., (1990) *How to Coach Swimming,* Collins-Willow

Cross R., (Edit.) (1991) *Swimming Teaching and Coaching – Level 1,* ASA

Eaton D., (Edit.) (1990) *Life Saving,* Royal Life Saving Society (UK)

Gleeson G., (Edit.) (1986) *The Growing Child in Competitive Sport,* Hodder & Stoughton and British Association of National Coaches

Hardy C., (1987) *Handbook for the Teacher of Swimming,* Pelham

Hardy C., (1989) *Let's Go Swimming,* Stanley Thornes

Harre D., (Edit.) (1982) *Principles of Sports Training – Introduction to the theory and methods of training,* Sportverlag Berlin

Hartmann and Tünnemann (1989) *Fitness and Strength Training,* Sportverlag Berlin

Hazeldine R., (1987) *Fitness for Sport,* Crowood Press

Institute of Baths & Recreation Management, (1990) *Diving into Swimming Pools,* IBRM

Knapp B., (1963) *Skill in Sport – the attainment of proficiency,* Routledge & Kegan Paul

Maglischo E., (1982) *Swimming Faster,* Mayfield Publishing Co

National Coaching Foundation, (1984) *Introductory Study Pack 1 The Coach in Action,* NCF

National Coaching Foundation, (1984) *Introductory Study Pack 2 The Body in Action,* NCF

National Coaching Foundation, (1984) *Introductory Study Pack 3 Safety and Injury,* NCF

National Coaching Foundation, (1984) *Introductory Study Pack 4 Improving Techniques,* NCF

National Coaching Foundation, (1984) *Introductory Study Pack 5 Mind Over Matter,* NCF

National Coaching Foundation, (1984) *Introductory Study Pack 6 Planning and Practice,* NCF

National Coaching Foundation, (1984) *Introductory Study Pack 7 Working with Children,* NCF

Burrows P., (1991) *Introductory Study Pack 8 Coaching People with Disability,* NCF

National Coaching Foundation, (1986) *Coaching Handbook 1 The Coach at Work,* NCF

National Coaching Foundation, (1986) *Coaching Handbook 2 Safety First for Coaches,* NCF

National Coaching Foundation, (1986) *Coaching Handbook 3 Physiology and Performance,* NCF

Oppenheim F., (1970) *The History of Swimming,* Swimming World

Pursley D., (1986) *Climb to the Top,* Aquazoid Publications

Sports Council, (1988) *Safety in Swimming Pools,* Sports Council/Health & Safety Commission

Verrier J., (1988) *Swimming,* The Crowood Press

Wellington P. & Cross C., (1992) *Nutrition for Swimming – your personal guide,* National Coaching Foundation

Wilke K., Madsen Ø., (1986) *Coaching the Young Swimmer,* Pelham Books

Wirhed R., (1984) *Athletic Ability and the Anatomy of Motion,* Wolfe Medical Publications

Wootton S., (1989) *Nutrition for Sport,* Simon & Schuster

ASA Information

ASA Handbook, ASA (Annual publication)

ASA Competitive Start Award, ASA Awards Centre

ASA Information Sheet 17, *National Registration*

ASA Information Sheet 18, *The Organisation of Swimming Clubs*

ASA Information Sheet 24, *Organising a Competition*

ASA leaflet, (1992) *It's Your Neck – Poolside diving safety advice*

Journals

Coaching Focus, published three times a year by NCF

Swimming Times, published monthly by Swimming Times Ltd, Address as for ASA

Published Papers

British Association of National Coaches (BANC), (1987) *The Growing Child in Competitive Sport,* BANC International Congress Proceedings

Cooke G., (Edit.) (1989) *The Growing Child in Competitive Sport,* British Institute of Sports Coaches (formerly BANC) International Congress Proceedings

Maglischo E., (1987) *British Swimming Coaches Association: The Ernie Maglischo Papers,* BSCA

THE ASA AWARDS SCHEME

Introduction

The *ASA Awards Scheme* is the most successful proficiency awards scheme in British Sport. The scheme has two major functions:

- to provide motivation to help encourage continued participation;
- to introduce pupils to a series of challenges and skills which become gradually more demanding.

Young children, particularly, are encouraged by success and this provides motivation for continued involvement in swimming and its associated disciplines. Badges and certificates are an ideal way of recognising achievement and holders of an ASA Award can be proud of their success.

Duckling Awards

These awards are designed to introduce very young children and their parents to the environment and pleasures of the water. There are three grades. The ASA recommends that children should be at least five months old and have completed their "triple injections".

Rainbow Awards

These are aimed at pupils of five years and older and are designed to demonstrate the pupils' ability to swim from A to B without pause and without stress.

- **Puffin Award**

  This award is designed for pre-school children and pupils with a disability. It is designed to test the pupils' ability to swim 5m using a buoyancy aid.

- **Other Rainbow Awards**

  These are made at 5m, 10m, 25m, 50m, 100m, 200m, 400m, 800m, 1,000m, 1,500m, 2,000m, 3,000m, 4,000m and 5,000m.

Water Skills Awards

Grades 1, 2 and 3 are a good foundation for the "early swimmer" and pupils with a disability. This scheme develops confidence and all-round skills in watermanship, and teaches pupils "How" and "Why" they move in water. Eventually skills required in competitive swimming, synchronised swimming, water polo and diving are introduced. The variety in these awards adds interest to swimming schemes and lessons.

National Curriculum (Water Skills) Awards

The Government has accepted the recommendation of the Physical Education Working Group that "all pupils should swim at least 25 metres and demonstrate an understanding of water safety" by the end of key stage 2 (11 years of age). This then becomes the Water Skills element of the award.

Swimming Challenge

In this scheme pupils are challenged to achieve targets for which they need an efficient performance using a wide range of skills. Stamina is also an important factor in the higher Awards of the series.

Personal Survival Awards

These awards change from time to time to take account of the latest research into immersion in cold water. Designed to educate, these are a must for every swim programme. It is essential that they are taught with imagination and as realistically as possible. They could provide opportunities and a sound basis for projects and assignments covering all areas of the curriculum.

Youth Swimming Awards

The *ASA Youth Swimming Award* is designed to provide an opportunity for young people of fourteen years of age and over to make an active and positive contribution to society. The aim of the award is to encourage young people to increase their knowledge and involvement in swimming, to swim for fitness and health, to encourage them to assist in the running of swimming clubs or events, and to help others to increase their swimming skills. The award is in three sections, Skill, Service and Safety. The three sections of the Award may be completed in any order and over any length of time.

Diving Skills Awards

These are designed to give pupils an early introduction to diving skills, this scheme will provide underwater confidence, body awareness and spring, preparing the diver to progress to advanced skills when working with a specialist diving teacher. These progressive awards are the perfect introduction to competitive diving.

Competitive Start Award (CSA)

It is the ASA's policy that swimmers should not be permitted to dive from a starting block of a maximum height of 500mm from the water surface into water of a minimum depth of 0.9m until they have demonstrated an ability to execute a shallow racing dive, in a consistent fashion, into water of at least full reach depth. The Competitive Start Award (CSA), and the teaching progressions leading to it, are intended to bring competitors to this standard of competence.

Speed Swimming Awards

With good teaching efficient strokes develop, which, in turn, enable pupils to swim further and faster. This scheme is intended to introduce pupils to the competitive scene.

Water Polo Awards

These awards have been carefully designed to introduce 6-12 year olds to the basic skills of the game. Each test builds on the skills of those preceding it.

Synchronised Swimming Awards

These have a creative bias and require a high level of control. They aim specifically to widen the swimmers' range of skills and are also suited to the swimmer who wishes to take up synchronised swimming.

Swimfit Awards

These are primarily designed to motivate adults to adopt a swimming programme by setting themselves achievement targets.

They have the following advantages:
- competitive swimmers may use it to log their training;
- it may be used to improve and maintain success by developing the cardio-respiratory system using speed and/or distance swims;
- when used regularly, it can contribute to a health and fitness programme suitable for all age groups.

The awards are cumulative so that the first one mile award may be counted towards the five miles award and so on. There are no time limits for these awards.

Ultimate Swimmer Award

This is awarded free of charge to those who achieve certain grades in various schemes and is designed to encourage pupils to experiment with a range of awards requiring a number of skills.

Information covering the whole *ASA Awards Scheme* may be obtained from the ASA Awards Centre on Freephone 0800 220292 or write to the ASA Awards Centre, 1 Kingfisher Enterprise Park, 50 Arthur Street, Redditch, Worcestershire, B98 8LG, telephone – 0527 514288, fax – 0527 514277.

NOTES ON THE CHAPTER AUTHORS

Jennifer Gray

Jennifer qualified as a teacher of Physical Education at Chelsea College of Human Movement. As a competitor she was a member of the first GB Synchronised Swimming team as well as being a diver of national standard. In 1975 she joined the ASA as a Development Officer, with special responsibilities for diving and synchronised swimming. Jennifer is an ASA Principal Tutor (Swimming) and a Senior Tutor for Synchronised swimming and Diving. She is currently a freelance swimming consultant. She is also the author of several books, including *Synchronised Swimming, a Complete Guide.*

Steve Greenfield

Steve is a former competitive swimmer at national level, and has been involved in coaching since the early 1980s. During his coaching career he has worked with swimmers from novice to national standard, both in England and the USA. He is currently working with Basingstoke Swimming Club, where he leads a team of 30 part-time and voluntary teachers and coaches. His club has recently produced its first national finalist. Steve is both an ASA Coach (Swimming) and Tutor (Swimming). He also coached for the Triathlon team when the sport was demonstrated as a possible new event at the Commonwealth Games. Steve is also a qualified Weight Training Coach and has acted as "strength" coach to athletes and soccer players.

Colin Hardy

Colin, who gained his PhD in 1992, is a Senior Lecturer in the Department of Physical Education, Sports Science and Recreation Management at Loughborough University. He has written three books on swimming and has had over 40 articles published in professional and academic journals. He has also presented papers at national and international conferences. Colin has been involved in teacher education since 1964 and, during that time, has been involved in many ASA teaching courses. The University Swimming and Water Polo squads have won numerous UAU championships during his 27 years as coach. He continues to swim regularly at Masters competitions, and constantly encourages others to participate in the sport.

Lynn Hogarth

Lynn has been involved in swimming for many years, initially as a competitive swimmer, then as a coach with City of Hull Swimming Club. In 1987 she formed the Hull Masters Swimming Club. In 1990 she moved to Cambridge as Swimming Development Manager, Cambridge City Council Services, and also as Coaching Representative for City of Cambridge Swimming Club. Lynn is an ASA Senior Tutor (Swimming Coaching) and an ASA Tutor (Swimming Teaching). She is also a member of the ASA Coach Certificate sub-committee and the Marketing and Publicity Officer for the Association of Swimming Development Officers (ASDO). Lynn regularly tutors at residential schools and presents a number of seminars on various swimming related topics.

Tony Holmyard

Tony trained at Loughborough as a Physical Education specialist and taught in Bristol Schools for six years. He followed this with two years as a National Technical Officer for the ASA. Currently he is a Lecturer in Physical Education at the University of Bristol, where his interests include all swimming disciplines, exercise and health studies and fitness training. Tony is an ASA Coach (Swimming) and Advanced Teacher (Swimming), a Principal Tutor (Teaching) and Senior Tutor (Coaching). He is a member of the ASA Coach Certificate and Masters Committees. Tony has written or contributed to several ASA publications, and is author of *A Guide to Masters Swimming*. He has wide interests in swimming from teaching young children to Senior Citizens, competing in Masters swimming and Water Polo. Tony is coach to the University of Bristol Swimming Club and Bristol Masters Swimming Club. He also has coaching and team managing experience at international level.

John Lawton

John completed his initial training as a teacher at Loughborough and then taught for 13 years, including six as Head of Physical Education at a large secondary school. During that time he also successfully completed an OU degree. He moved to America to teach Physical Education to primary age pupils, later returning to the UK to study for a second degree, an MSc in Sports Science, at Loughborough. John then joined the Leicestershire Education Authority as a Physical Education Adviser. He is currently the ASA Director of Education. He has always been heavily involved in the teaching and coaching of swimming and is an ASA Advanced Teacher (Swimming), an ASA Coach (Swimming) and an ASA Tutor.

Colin Lee

Colin is former competitive swimmer and water polo player and has taught swimming for some 25 years. He trained as a teacher of Physical Education at Goldsmiths' College, later gaining his B.Ed degree at St Pauls College, Cheltenham, and his PhD at the University of London. He taught for 10 years in primary schools in London and Bath, and followed this by becoming Head of Physical Education at Bath College of Higher Education. Colin has carried out extensive research into skill acquisition by young children and lectures to several major organisations on this topic. Since leaving higher education in 1991 he has combined business interests with freelance consultancy. The latter has specialised in developing the practical application of theories of skill learning in sports coaching, general teaching and commercial environments. He is also a Staff Tutor with the National Coaching Foundation.

Ian Oliver

Ian has been the Swimming Development Officer to the City of Newcastle since 1978. He is Chief Coach to the City of Newcastle ASC and has played a large part in developing it into a strong force in British Swimming. The Club has produced many internationals, including an Olympic swimmer. Ian started coaching whilst studying Physical Education at Madeley College in the mid-sixties. After qualifying as a Physical Education teacher he became Head of Physical Education at Rutherford School, Newcastle, and, during his time there in the 1970s, the school became one of the leading names in school swimming in the country. He is one of the England senior team coaches, and was Chief Coach to the England Youth (Intermediate) Squad during 1989-92. Ian has been a member of the ASA Swimming Committee since 1986 and has been heavily involved in the restructuring of the National Age Group programme.

Carl Payton

Carl Payton completed a BA(Hons) degree in Human Movement Studies and a Post Graduate Certificate of Education at the University of Wales. He later gained an MSc in Physical Education and Sports Science from Loughborough University. He currently lectures in sports biomechanics and swimming at the Manchester Metropolitan University, Crewe & Alsager Faculty Sport and Exercise Science Research and Development Unit, and is conducting PhD research into the three dimensional underwater pull patterns of competitive swimmers. Carl is a former British Students' Freestyle Champion, a UAU Water Polo player and coach to Loughborough Town Swimming Club. He is now a keen Masters swimmer.

Michael Peyrebrune

Michael was an international Back Crawl swimmer for Scotland and Great Britain between 1984-1990. He gained degree in Human Movement Studies from the Cardiff Institute of Higher Education in 1986 and then, in 1989, he completed a Masters Degree in Sports Science at Loughborough University. He now lectures and researches in physiological aspects of swimming in the Department of Physical Education, Sports Science and Recreation Management at Loughborough University. Michael is a qualified ASA Coach (Swimming) and has been coach and Head Coach to the university swimming team during the last four years. His latest appointment is as a coach to the British student swimming team for the 1993 World Student Games in Buffalo. He continues to maintain his links between the theoretical and practical aspects of swimming training through articles and lectures. Michael has also been involved in the construction of a Sports Science testing programme for British swimming.

Trevor Thomas

Trevor became involved in swimming as a parent in 1955, and embarked on the usual teacher/coach qualification "treadmill". He is active in teaching/coaching and administration, as well as being Team Manager to various England swimming teams, including the 1986 Commonwealth Games. Trevor is an ASA Tutor and Principal Tutor (Swimming), and has served on Education Committees from club to national level. He also has served on the Visual Aids and Publications Working Party, in which capacity he was jointly responsible for the detailed production of several reprints of *The Teaching of Swimming* publication. Trevor has served on the ASA Swimming Committee, the ASA and the ASFGB Committees. He is an experienced tutor/examiner of ASA swimming officials, a FINA list referee and starter, officiating at all levels, including the European Championships and the Seoul Olympic Games. He was president of the ASA in 1988.